THE GREAT ECONOMIC TRAIN WRECK

When America Went Off the Rails

T0145913

THE GREAT
ECONOMIC
TRAIN
WRECK

When America
Went Off the Rails

How the Nation's
Financial Crisis
Looks from Main St.

KEVIN H. CLARK

FOREWORD BY PETE HOEKSTRA

Advantage®

Published by Advantage, Charleston, South Carolina.
Member of Advantage Media Group.

ADVANTAGE is a registered trademark and the Advantage colophon is a trademark of Advantage Media Group, Inc.

Printed in the United States of America.

ISBN: 978-1-59932-281-0
LCCN: 2011916626

This publication is designed to provide accurate and authoritative information in regard to the subject matter covered. It is sold with the understanding that the publisher is not engaged in rendering legal, accounting, or other professional services. If legal advice or other expert assistance is required, the services of a competent professional person should be sought.

Advantage Media Group is proud to be a part of the Tree Neutral® program. Tree Neutral offsets the number of trees consumed in the production and printing of this book by taking proactive steps such as planting trees in direct proportion to the number of trees used to print books. To learn more about Tree Neutral, please visit www.treeneutral.com. To learn more about Advantage's commitment to being a responsible steward of the environment, please visit www.advantagefamily.com/green

Advantage Media Group is a leading publisher of business, motivation, and self-help authors. Do you have a manuscript or book idea that you would like to have considered for publication? Please visit www.amgbook.com or call 1.866.775.1696

First books are birthed more than written. Like a birth, this book,

My first endeavor at putting thoughts to page could only

Be accomplished with love and support of a gracious family.

I dedicate this book to my wife, Jane, who allowed me the space—

to think, to dream and ultimately write.

To my children, Chris, Aaron and Matt who

lived with morning rituals of reading and radio shows.

Thank you for the inspiration your love and support provided.

Acknowledgements

This book is a culmination of hours of work and editing. For two years, I have been fortunate to have the able assistance of Tiffany Graham, Jenna Hunger and Stephanie Smith who were kind enough to help me prepare the weekly radio shows with candor and a sense of humor. Red Kingman has been the perfect host of the "Kevin Clark Business Minute" on 1450 am WHTC radio. His engaging conversations and wit have made it a lively discussion week after week, on topical economical issues.

I want to thank the team at Advantage Media for their creative approach to a distinctive and personal project. I especially would like to thank my editor, Denis Boyles who had a unique vision and belief in this project and the story I would ultimately tell.

Foreword

America's in an anxious mood. It's an anxiety based on ambiguity and the feeling that as a nation we now seem almost leaderless and uncertain of where we're headed. The divide between the "elites" of the political class and grass-roots activists has widened. From America's Main Streets, Washington looks more and more like a foreign country where people do things differently because they think about things differently, and where distant financial "experts" are in command of a trench warfare they don't have to fight. From the foxholes, it doesn't always appear the strategy of the moment is working very well.

The past three years have seen an avalanche of policies that have made the differences between Pennsylvania Avenue and Main Street greater than ever. Inside Washington's beltway, we measure these differences by polls and by the calls and notes we get from faraway constituents. But those don't always tell the full story. To see how America measures these differences, you have to look at the cities and towns, where jobs, friendships, hopes and common sense tell a story that's not at all like the story told in Washington.

The Great Economic Train Wreck is what Kevin Clark calls the years that followed from the economic emergencies of 2008 and the effect of the policies put in place since then to try to address the country's financial distress. Through 2009 and 2010, in his weekly radio broadcasts, he provided a clear picture of how it felt to live life in the cities and towns of middle America. Now, revisited in hindsight, we can see how much there is to learn from an eyewitness to the derailing of the country's finances.

You'll recognize in this book, as I did, the life of your community, the lives of your friends and family, the life of a country that sometimes seems invisible from Washington. It's a series of snapshots that show how one bad idea can lead to another, and how inventive, positive men and women survive bad times. It shows how far political decisions have taken us off-course and left the country wondering what to do next, and it shows how clear-thinking in a financial foxhole on the front lines of economic policy can sometimes be an art.

But it's not a pessimistic book. In fact, what *The Great Economic Train Wreck* shows us most of all is that by learning from our most recent mistakes, we can come up with smarter, better ways to get us all back on track again.

−Pete Hoekstra

Introduction

When the trouble started, I started to personalize my fear – what would I do if I lost my job, my retirement funds, could I survive? My mind was racing as only the unpredictable and uncontrollable will cause. I was running through the disaster scenarios, catastrophizing step by step – with each thought seemingly more dire than before and each thought more hopeless than before. I have learned panic attacks will do that. It is safe to say I was having a personal dilemma of "fight" or "flight" and "flight" was looking quite attractive. Despite my brief bouts with denial, it became clear to me that this event was greater than the moment. I simply wasn't ready to grasp the complexity of it.

I was vacationing in Florida, walking the beautiful powdered sand beach of Bonita as I thought about the news of March 14, 2008, which would be the first major string to unravel: The venerable Wall Street banking firm of Bear Stearns received an emergency infusion of capital from JP Morgan Chase. Surely, this was an isolated event? The Federal Reserve told us the sub-prime mortgage issues were contained – this was an anomaly, right? We would soon learn that the capital for Bear Stearns would not be sufficient for continuing operations, and for $2 a share, the company was sold.

There are times when you simply know events are out of control and the slide is not over; you can tell by the anxiousness in the pit of your stomach. My experience and anxiousness was impressing on me that Bear Stearns was not a random misstep for the investment banking firm, and I questioned myself as to what was I missing.

What I was missing was the realization that the U.S. economy and financial markets were beginning to falter in ways very few people could comprehend. The systemic breakdown of our credit markets would have interconnected consequences that would eventually touch all of us and leave us here in 2011 quite weary. How often did I catch myself thinking "if I only would have known"; six simple words, and millions thought them and still seem haunted by them.

I began my career as a financial advisor in 1982. I taught high school government and economics for three years prior to that and lived through the last great recession of 1980-81. Those were the days of America's "malaise" and the hope for a better and brighter tomorrow was brought in by a new, confident president. Over the next two decades, we indeed would experience the greatest bull market in history and, like so often happens, we would lose track of the consequence of misguided public policy and attain an under-appreciation for market risk.

I have spent nearly 30 years working in the financial services industry and have had thousands of interactions with clients about their hopes, dreams and sometimes fears as I planned and guided them toward their financial goals. I have been and remain hopeful that freedom will cover both a multitude of public policy sins and the sheer greed that has resulted from the ethical breakdown of corporate America. Our history seems peppered with portions of both.

Yet, free people will ultimately persevere; and that is why when we come so close to calamity, we somehow find a way to pull together. I firmly believe it's foolish to sell the American people short – they are the ultimate value stock. But only time will tell if this crisis is different.

The mortgage crisis breached the levee of financial containment when the mortgage giants FNMA (Fannie Mae) and Freddie Mac disclosed massive losses and the government backing of those enterprises was brought into question. With this systemic failure the confidence of investors, traders and market insiders was slipping away. The average investor seemed scared and bewildered as market events were moving too fast for thoughtful reflection on current events.

Oil prices would spike to $140 per barrel in July of 2008, and with the presidential election coming into the home stretch, divisive political rhetoric was rising and the fragility of the U.S. and world credit and monetary systems seemed to be undetectable or at least lost in the noise of a campaign.

By early September, the markets had become somewhat range-bound with the classic characteristics of a bear market: a market that would rally but not be able to sustain an advance. The media were having a feeding frenzy as the presidential election resembled more of a reality TV show as the charisma of Barack Obama was being challenged by the Republican vice presidential candidate, Sarah Palin.

I remember looking for some kind of historical precedent to help explain events, as confidence was teetering on panic, and the sheer weight of trillions of dollars worth of bad debt was about to consume our financial system. The data points seemed to be pointing toward the Great Depression, and yet the layers of denial were so thick it was clearly impossible for the average person to predict the devastation to follow.

The week of September 15, 2008, would inevitably be the one, in retrospect, in which the economy was broken and the financial markets were trying to assess the damage. This time, three financial titans collapsed: Lehman Brothers, Merrill Lynch and AIG; the dominos fell. This was unthinkable, and for investors, the idea of these companies falling like dominos brought on high anxiety and a growing panic that our financial system could be on the cliff teetering toward total collapse.

For the past 25 years I have been hosting a weekly analysis dissecting the markets and economy for our local radio station. How do you remain positive when the world seems out of control? Here's what I said that September, *"This is a treacherous short-term market. Markets have a hard time dealing with uncertainty. Right now we do not know the inter-connectedness of the collapse and failures of these companies. For the average investor, you should be very careful; we don't know what we don't know."*

Little did I know how true that statement would become.

It's difficult to capture the loss of confidence and eroding hope most Americans were feeling. Again, those familiar words came rushing back "if I had only known" – but we didn't, and we had to move forward bruised and shaken.

On September 20, I was overwhelmed, frustrated and angry as events seemed to be washing away so many hopes and dreams. It was a Saturday, and after reading through the paper I decided to write a letter to my clients to express how I was feeling about the world as I saw it.

The American people have endured quite a week. The loss of money, although billions, pales in relation to the loss of faith in a financial system we take for granted. Peggy Noonan wrote an op-ed in the WSJ titled "Why the campaign will get mean" and painted a melancholy picture of what could have been. There is a deep distrust of the media and a deeper distrust of Washington. There is something about "bail outs" that leaves you empty. But, at the end of the day you can't bail out character – you either have it or you don't.

In this sad episode of American history, the failure of our national moral compass leaves us all melancholy, wondering how did we get here? The two campaigns talk of change, talk about what they will do to make America strong again. I would rather hear about America being good again. Our strength is in our goodness, our sense of right and wrong. The campaign is surely turning mean and Ms. Noonan captured it well.

My hope in this campaign will not come from the press, which has betrayed the public trust, or from political leaders, who simply failed to lead, but rather from the collective wisdom of Main Street. It is on Main Street where common sense and judgment resides. It is Main Street that over the years has made America strong. You can't bail out character; I just hope Main Street still has it. I hope the wisdom of Main Street can see through the marketing of false hopes and wild dreams and sees an America that still can be great. As Americans we must expect better and demand more; after all it's a nation of the people. Come November we will vote. My simple prayer is: I hope Main Street shows up.

We now know many people showed up and the resulting shift in political policy and philosophy was just beginning.

Historians and economists will write volumes on the reasoning for the extraordinary government intervention that took place in the last week in September of 2008. On October 3, 2008, President George W. Bush would sign into law the Troubled Asset Relief Program – better referred to as TARP. Although most likely this program will be seen in the years to come as a necessary government action at the time, the negative momentum of fear and panic was too great to be contained by this massive government intervention.

As we closed out 2008, it was hard to find historical parallels, short of war or pandemic, that adequately described our financial dilemma. With weeks before the presidential inauguration, credible leadership was missing. Confidence in Congress had sunk to nearly single-digit poll numbers and, despite the high voter turnout for the presidential election, having a political and leadership novice at the helm of our government was not comforting to Wall Street.

My hope is that as you read through my weekly commentaries you will be informed from a unique perspective and, hopefully, entertained by the anecdotes and modern parables I have woven in.

This two-year journey will undoubtedly be a time that will forever change our nation and jade current investors for years to come. The failure of government leaves one shaken. The trust and the hope for the American Way wavers when corrupted by political power. That is happening; it is disturbing and demands action. Never perfect, history suggests that the next response may be that ordinary people will emerge as the heroes in the years to come – people using common sense, who simply want a better future for their children and grandchildren.

The road to recovery will be an extended journey; for some it will be their lifetime and for others it will be decades in the future before the experience is diluted. Spending my adult life in the financial industry, I now have a much deeper appreciation for the children of the Great Depression. For years, I would hear from investors stories of loss, stories that, when I watched their eyes, I would see that thousand-yard stare and I would hear words that depict what today we call "austerity."

Although with deep nuance, "austerity" was not a mere word – it was a way of life, a hard life, a lean life where common dreams of a bright future were muted by circumstance – and I always listened intently trying to capture the essence of the psychology that shaped the attitude of the investor who sat across the table from me. Sometimes there were tears; the whitewater of turbulent times continues to weigh heavily on their mind and memory.

The remnants of the Great Crash of 1929 echoed for generations, and in those stories it was becoming evident to me that the financial crash of 2008 would reverberate for decades as well, connecting generations to come with the despondency that national trauma will forge.

The historical playback you will read in the pages ahead are the attempt to find perspective and context for investors today. My words then and my reflections now will, I hope, help to put your own experiences in a frame.

My hope is you will take a little ownership of what is written and add your own thoughts in the margins. I believe the story of what is happening to us is still not written, but in the fullness of time and generations to come your children and children's children will want to know – they will want to know how we made it through. And they will listen for the echoes you may have written in the margins of this book.

–Kevin Clark
Holland, Michigan

CHAPTER
1

December 24, 2008

DJIA: 8,419.49
S&P: 863.16

So Why Am I Hopeful?

Housing continues to plague a short-term rally for the U.S. economy. Investors should expect news to continue to be negative. You should expect negative GDP for the fourth quarter 2008 and you should expect unemployment to increase an additional 2%-3%. We should also expect corporate earnings to remain weak in the first couple quarters of 2009. Clearly, the cloud of pessimism will be with us for a while.

However...I believe there is a tremendous amount of bad news priced into this market. With this much pessimism...there may be reasons to be optimistic.

I am encouraged, albeit cautiously, that despite continued negative news, stocks are leveling off, and conditions seem to be improving for the markets.

Have a wonderful Christmas...

Heading into December of 2008 unemployment was rising quickly, as industry after industry contracted, accelerating the recession we had begun many months before. At 7.1%, unemployment had risen from the 4.8% level just prior to the collapse of Bear Stearns.

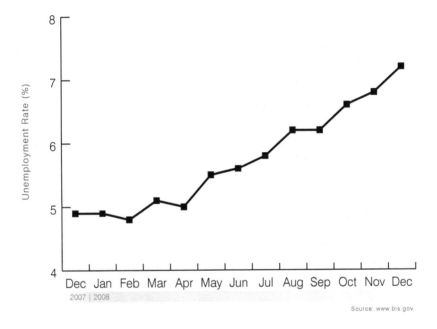

Source: www.bis.gov

March 1993 was the last time we had seen unemployment at this 7% level; we collectively were holding our breath, hoping the worst might be over for us. However, we all knew better.

December 31, 2008

DJIA: 8,668.39
S&P: 890.64

Weekly Update

On this last day of 2008, I think we can say, "Finally, this year is over." The record books will also show this to be the third worst market in U.S. history. With all of the negative economic news out there, I'm sure poor performance is expected. In fact, the Dow Jones Average is down 35% and the S&P 500 is down 39% year to date. However, despite the negative news, stocks seem poised to attempt a near-term rally. That would be welcomed by us all.

My final point this morning is, until the credit markets begin to normalize I don't think we will see a sustainable rally in the stock market as well as the economy. With the unprecedented government stimulus on the horizon, it looks like 2009 will see credit markets begin this process.

I found this quote by John Templeton that I believe is appropriate today:

"The most costly errors in selecting stocks are made by people whose thinking is dominated by the question of the temporary short-term trend of earnings." (June 1949)

Keeping a long-term perspective in mind can be challenging in times like these.

As we now know, the employment picture would worsen and continue rising into the end of the year. Although employment was a key issue, it would be the credit markets that needed time to heal.

Finally, the year was coming to a close. It had been a most memorable and difficult year for most of us. The normal anticipation of the holiday season was muted for me, and I remember thinking that history was filled with such somber times, yet we somehow managed. As I reflect back on my thoughts, the 2008 Christmas season would be a message of transition.

Transitions can be an adventure; some are mysteries and others capture a raw emotion, the kind that only trauma creates. We all have transitions and, without a doubt, they can be positive, but "transition" implies leaving something behind; that will leave you reminiscent, looking back and longing for more or denying the pain. I caught myself thinking "if I only would have known," realizing that this would be a generational regret, a passage from one American to the next and more than my own personal regrets.

It's interesting, that on that Christmas, I was sensing the profound changes to come, not only for my own family, but for the nation. I felt the grief of losing something precious already seeping into my soul. Like an early morning fog that runs like a stream in the deep valleys, this fog of loss would begin in the depths of our thoughts and losses to grow and obstruct our view of tomorrow.

Christmas 2008 would be bittersweet. It would be a tentative joy for most, and the security of spending time with family would begin to fade. With the cold winter months looming on the horizon of 2009, the brutal reality of our circumstances was scrolling along the bottom of the evening news and a sense of despair was leaching into our national psyche.

CHAPTER
2

January 8, 2009

DJIA: 9,015.10
S&P: 934.70

Weekly Update

The Wall Street Journal this morning reported the stock markets here in the U.S. and around the world have rallied since the November lows. The Dow Jones is up 19.4%. The S&P 500 is up more than 24%.

How can that be with all the bad news: Wood Asset Management released a report in which it believes that cash is at an 18-year high, with $8.85 trillion held in cash. (Yes, I said Trillion.) That amount of cash is equal to 74% of the value of all publicly traded stocks. This is the highest ratio since 1990. This ratio jumped 86% in 2008, the biggest increase since the Fed began keeping records in 1959. With all the cash on the sidelines I continue to believe this is not a crisis of liquidity, but rather a crisis of confidence.

Let's look at a few numbers:

$8.85 trillion in cash on the sidelines

$700 billion government TARP program

Proposed $1 trillion stimulus plan

Proposed tax cuts

$200 billion annualized savings from falling gasoline prices

When does this recession end?

I don't know...but, we do know the fuel necessary for a recovery is available. Confidence will take time to rebuild.

As confidence was being wrung out of the U.S. consumer, the headlines would read that the Conference Board reported consumer confidence had again declined for the month of January. The Conference Board index registered the lowest level since its inception in 1967. At the same time, we were beginning to notice the trillions of dollars accumulating on the sidelines, demonstrating how the shock of the economic trauma was becoming entrenched.

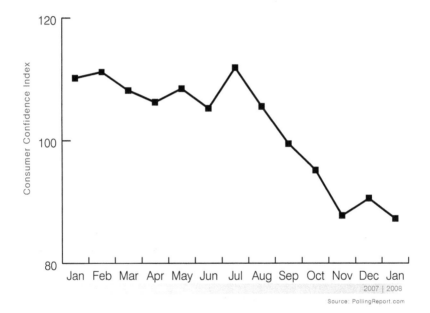

Source: PollingReport.com

January 14, 2009

DJIA: 8,448.56

S&P: 871.79

Weekly Update
_____

Here are some numbers from this morning:

MBA mortgage applications +15.8%

Bloomberg global confidence index 8.72 vs. 6.07 last month

Advance retail sales -2.7% vs. expected -1.2%

Less autos -3.1% vs. expected -1.4%

Since last week, the data point that sticks out is energy prices. Last week. West Texas Intermediate crude was at $48.55. A 25% drop in crude.

An observation:

The longer the markets trade lower or in a narrow range, the more the average investor experiences "bear market fatigue." Remember, since 1949, on average the S&P 500 has started moving up 5.4 months before the end of a recession. The average gain has been more than 20% for those 5.4 months. In the 1973-74 period, the numbers are 7 months and 40%. History would suggest patience will be rewarded.

I noticed clients becoming weary with the extreme volatility. I would call this "bear market fatigue," and with confidence rapidly eroding, people were scared and unsettled. Once again, I heard people saying that stock phrase: "If I only had known." This sentiment resided in the back of the minds of most investors, always questioning their own decisions and creating an added layer of anxiety.

January 21, 2009

DJIA: 7,949.09
S&P: 805.22

The Inflection Point of Fear and Fact

Yesterday, we had a day of hope and optimism filling Washington, D.C. However, we also had a day of despair on Wall Street, as major banks declined more than 20%. What a day indeed yesterday was.

Politics is front and center in the banking system as the uncertainty over the role of government in the U.S. banking system plays out. Policymakers have a difficult task of finding the right balance between appropriate assistance and further intrusion. The decline in bank stocks yesterday highlights the fear of "what could be" in dire times. This makes for very emotional trading. However, here is a fact: IBM ($81.98) reported a 12% rise in fourth-quarter earnings and gave a favorable outlook for 2009.

History has told us that at these points of inflection between fear and facts, investors have had historic opportunities.

Yesterday we saw another record. From the election of Barack Obama in November through the inauguration yesterday, the DJIA declined a record 14%. The second-largest drop of 13% was 1932-33 with the election of FDR. I point this out because following the drop in 1933, the market rallied 75%. When fear and facts come together, something is about to happen.

From employment woes to consumer confidence crashing, the headlines now were redirected toward the banking industry. Panic-selling days were becoming common place, and a sense of towel-throwing seemed close at hand. Although we had no way of knowing how serious the discussions were, there was talk of the U.S. banking industry being nationalized. This was unthinkable. Only by going back to the Great Depression could we recall such drastic measures. But that news was on the table, and most of us braced for the banking stress test results that the Treasury Department was requiring to gauge the capital strength of our largest banks.

January 28, 2009

DJIA: 8,174.73
S&P: 845.71

$900 Billion Dollars: Stimulus or Spending?

It is widely expected that the House of Representatives will pass the largest and most expensive spending bill in history. It is unclear how much this bill will accomplish in terms of immediate stimulus to the economy. The good news...policymakers understand there is a need for an economic stimulus package. The bad news...partisanship will sink the plan unless we see strong leadership that is balanced toward compromise.

Stay tuned...it's your money.

When politics drives Wall Street, expect a bumpy ride. It is very difficult for investors to trust politicians. There is a reason Congress has a 10% approval rating.

It had been a tumultuous week, with little stability showing up in day to day trading. It was unimaginable to believe we would see the U.S. banking system collapse and through congressional action be restructured through nationalization. Yet, in the panic of the moment, anything seemed possible.

The rational part of me knew that with increasing risk and panic, there would be the inevitable "great opportunity" for investors to begin buying the sell-offs; after all, we were seeing substantial discounts in terms of valuations.

But beyond our imaginations, I think most Americans found disturbing the realization that what existed as America six months before was gone. It had been replaced by a new reality. It was a national nightmare, and we were not waking up. In the desperate attempt to revive a comatose economy, Congress would pass the largest spending bill in U.S. history. The numbers were numbing to our senses, as billions gave way to trillions and the federal debt clock spun madly.

It was a new year, yet the markets continued to fall, as many investors could not shake the sense of doom that dominated the news. It was as though the markets were hyperventilating – desperately gasping for air, which seemed to be adding to the extreme measures of stress the nation was experiencing.

I remember sitting with my journal trying to describe in words what I was feeling – what was happening.

The day is beginning – though cloudy, dawn has begun and the sky starts to show signs of light. It's cold, very cold, as the wintry grip of January has a frozen touch on us. Life just moves slower in the cold. The days are short, and darkness seems to be ever-present. We are in dire times – dire in the sense of being outside of our recent experiences. So much wisdom has been found to be pure folly.

We were certainly witnessing history in the making, as the markets were tossed and turned by continual uncertainty. Fear was the constant thread running through the fabric of our economy. The nightmare continued as desperate measures were tangled in the web of politics, shredding our confidence.

CHAPTER
3

February 4, 2009

DJIA: 8,078.36
S&P: 838.51

Vital Optimism

When investors are confronted by confusion, uncertainty and financial pain, the natural temptation is to flee the market. This is often described as "bear market fatigue." It is no wonder we are looking at close to $10 trillion on the sidelines. Looking at the two-year Treasury yield at .94%, we know money on the sidelines is making virtually nothing.

What creeps into the investors' psyche is the concept of "It is different this time." However, the past shows a different story. History suggests that now is the time to average your way from the sidelines to the market; consider your risk tolerance, your long-term objective, and buy shares on a regular basis.

Great nations have an attitude of "vital optimism;" a quality of spirit possessed by a nation, community or person in which there is a persuasion that the best is yet to be. Throughout the 1930s, the war years of the 40s, or the 1973-74 oil embargo and recession, it was being said, "It's different this time" or "America had seen its best days," just like we are hearing today. I don't believe this is true. Do I know what the market will do in the short run? No... but I do believe America will overcome, and history would say to invest in America when you are confused, uncertain, and feeling economic pain.

Was it possible that our nation's best days were behind us? Had America seen its worldwide influence and economic prowess begin to decline, just as so many empires had throughout history? I don't believe we can know at this point if the America we all have yearned for will indeed be our future. What I do know is that in our history there have been numerous times when the overwhelming evidence was of decline, yet, despite our hardships, we had found a way to persevere and advance!

February 11, 2009

DJIA: 7,888.88
S&P: 827.16

All Roads Leading to Inflation?

After weeks of speculation as to the details of the new bank bailout program, the announcement left Wall Street with more questions than answers. What we always know is that uncertainty invites sellers into a market, and we certainly saw that yesterday. In an environment where public policy plays a major role in the financial markets, private investors are forced to wait on the sidelines for clarification on what the new policy means. The treasury's bank recovery program may in fact be good policy. However, in the short run, the devil is in the details. The one detail we are sure about is the size of this program. With the stimulus package working its way through Congress on top of the new Treasury program, we could be looking at more than $2 trillion of spending. We know from Economics 101 that more dollars chasing fewer goods and services leads to inflation. This $2 trillion in the short run is replacing the wealth that has been destroyed in the past few months. However, as the economy recovers and wealth once again is created and grows, the question still remains: What will happen to that $2 trillion?

I think it is important to start thinking about what will happen in 2010. With our current economic crisis and the possible cure being massive amounts of government money going into the system, those investments that perform well during times of rising prices should be considered for part of a portfolio. Keep watching the commodity prices and the 30 year Treasury yield. Many times they forecast future inflation.

The selling on Wall Street continued unabated. The political uncertainty became suffocating, forcing investors to remain cautious, waiting for better opportunities to re-enter the markets. With Congress exploding the budget deficit to historic levels in what would become a failed attempt at economic stimulus, many observers began to question how this newly created debt would be structured. Clearly, we had entered uncharted waters in terms of fiscal policy.

February 18, 2009

DJIA: 7,552.60
S&P: 789.17

Investors Voted With Their Feet

Late last week we were hoping for government support and a stimulus plan that would stabilize the banking system and help to reignite the U.S. economy... What we got was government induced uncertainty that has left investors skeptical. We still do not have specifics of the banking plan announced last week, and it may be weeks before we see how the government intends to spend $800 billion. What we do know is that investors voted with their feet and simply sold stocks, as a vote of no-confidence.

Here's my take: Despite the public policy miscues and mis-communications, our new administration will find a way to muddle through. At the end of the day, $800 billion will be added to the U.S. economy through the stimulus plan. Is this sufficient to save the economy? I think it is enough to stabilize the patient and keep it comfortable. I would expect to see another stimulus package in the area of $500 billion later this year. That should help move the economy forward.

In the short run, the banking system needs to stabilize, and of course housing needs to improve. I think we are in the trough of the recession and do believe with the markets struggling that dollar cost-averaging into solid U.S. companies is appropriate. Remember, there are trillions of dollars on the sidelines, and when they start to move into the markets, we could see upside volatility.

In the confusion of political and economic cross-currents, many of us were searching for a bottom to this market. On one particular evening, I found myself sitting down and reflecting in my journal on the day that had passed.

> *Another dreadful day in the market, with the Dow Jones averages falling to a six-year low; I find the amount of wealth destroyed in the past six months as truly staggering.*

Remarkably, we would experience an additional decline of 15%, and the nation would watch in quiet horror.

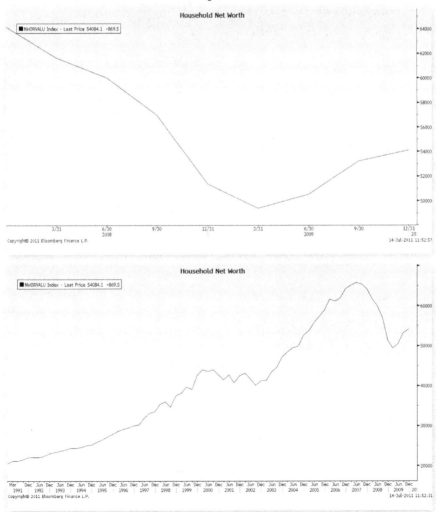

February 25, 2009

DJIA: 7,350.94
S&P: 773.14

It Will Take More Than One Speech

Last night, President Obama addressed a joint session of Congress and he tried to regain control of an agenda and reverse his downbeat rhetoric on the economy. He certainly communicated clearly that it was time to believe in America. However, it will take more than one speech to convince the markets that they can trust these new policies.

So...what do investors do now? You will need to believe one of two things about our economy. (1.) It is fundamentally strong and will recover, or (2.) It is fundamentally broken and will collapse. If you believe in recovery, than you should consider buying American assets: stocks, bonds and real estate. If you believe our best days are behind us, buy gold and sell stocks. Either way, a proper strategy is to do this gradually and dollar-cost-average in or out.

As for me, I believe in the U.S. economy and I believe in a recovery (despite ourselves). There is a saying that I continue to hold true, and that is, "Never bet against the American people."

As the world was seemingly unraveling before our eyes, we collectively held our breath as President Obama addressed a joint session of Congress. In an atmosphere of high anxiety, we had to assess the words of our president and weigh what we observed in our everyday lives. For investors, this speech presented a crossroads of sorts, as the deeply oversold markets were as shattered as history had shown after the crash of 1929.

How do you climb out of the economic rubble we had created since September? I clearly remember there was a sense of resignation as the markets became unhinged from economic fundamentals and common sense; panic will do that. I was hopeful; yet, my own words would betray the confidence I tried to portray. I wrote:

> *There is a song that Don McLean made famous; I hear the lyrics, "the day the music died. And they'll be singing, 'Bye, bye Miss American Pie.' drove my Chevy to the levee, but the levee was dry."*

I realize my music has died, my levee is dry. When you reach such a moment, there is this realization of your mortality and that the world is indeed dangerous. There is great questioning and great blame for why your music dies. I don't know what the days ahead will bring. I have little control over how this world will spin. I am not the center of the world – I am the leaf in autumn, struggling to keep from becoming dust.

Discouragement was at epidemic levels; it has always seemed unfamiliar territory for America, but we would move forward, and, from afar, you could see the fabric of modern politics fray dangerously. Things seemed to be coming apart, deepening the discouragement many Americans felt.

The President and Congress began to push an agenda for health care and climate change, rather than address the critical employment picture, which would be the number one issue for most Americans. This disconnect from the people and their paramount fear over lost jobs and tumbling home prices has brought us to the failing job approval ratings of both the President and Congress.

CHAPTER
4

March 4, 2009   DJIA: 6,726.02
                                       S&P: 696.33

Are We There Yet?

The direction of a bear market is always difficult to predict, and nearly impossible to know the bottom. The heightened pessimism becomes unrelenting, and ultimately people in the media will find at least one expert who will tell us that the Dow Jones will fall to nearly zero and that the world is going to end.

On the political front, we continue to have a smokescreen that prevents investors from seeing clearly. Numerous new proposals with few details, government spending increases, and a sense of high taxation leaves us wondering how this will affect our future. Issues like bank bailouts, national healthcare, and carbon cap-and-trade proposals make it difficult to see 2010, but I believe that there are positive signs pointing to the future that we cannot yet see.

Having said that, it has been an ugly week for stocks. Like traveling to a vacation spot, the question remains: Are we there yet? Have we reached our destination of the bottom? Raymond James' chief market strategist, Jeff Saut, believes 95% of the bear market is in, and that the only thing left to see is if the market bottoms with a whimper or a bang. Either way, the long-term investor should start thinking about 2010. Looking at indicators, which are showing the markets are oversold at levels similar to October's and November's, it seems as if this week could establish a near-term low. In a time where the average investor becomes anxious, discouraged and panicked, remember to be prepared for oversold opportunities.

March would come in like a lion. The barrage of selling would best be described as shock and awe. As we plummeted below the 7,000 level for the Dow Jones Index, opportunities were developing, providing a profit bonanza for those who believed we were near the bottom and the U.S. economy would in fact survive and grow again.

March 11, 2009

DJIA: 6,926.49
S&P: 719.60

What Is On the Other Side?

I received an e-mail last night from a client who is concerned about the economy, scared of the market, and confused as to what to do. I think most people share that sentiment - terrified to be in the market, yet terrified to be out. My client went on to say that he was going to hope for the best on the other side.

I continue to wonder, what does the other side look like? The high anxiety of the last two months has brought us tremendous irrationality in this market (stocks and bonds). However, I do not believe that this will be a long-lived episode in American history. Yesterday's market shows us how explosive a rally can be, despite how we feel, and tells us that the markets will become more rational over time.

How will we know if yesterday's rally will be sustained? Did we hit the bottom? I don't know the answers to those questions. Conditions for a strong rally are present - but just like a winter storm warning that may leave a foot of snow or none at all, we do not yet know what the current rally will do.

We do know that the banks must be stabilized and housing must improve. And with $2 trillion in new spending, the other side is becoming clearer... Trillions of new dollars chasing goods and services are the conditions needed to re-inflate this economy...

Is it possible to print $2 trillion and not see at least a momentary blip in economic activity? It appeared as though the beginning of the end for the great collapsing stock market was finally reached. Skepticism of any rally for stocks was running deep.

March 18, 2009

DJIA: 7,395.70
S&P: 778.12

Fact or Fizzle?

Last week, we discussed conditions being right for a market rally. The market has, in fact, rallied 6.7% since last Wednesday, and 13% since the low of 10 days ago. This rally has been welcomed, as most investors have been quite discouraged, but the question remains: Is this just a rally in a bear market, or something more substantial? In other words, is this fact or fizzle?

It has been a traumatic six months of wealth destruction, truly historic in proportion. But we should look beyond the moment and ask ourselves a few questions: (1.) Has my risk profile changed? (2.) Has my time horizon changed? (3.) Do I believe that the American economy will survive?

We have learned through this crisis that there is much we simply don't know. The risks we thought we understood were simply underestimated as we learned about credit default swaps and counter-party risk of massive proportions. We have also begun to understand the political risk to the markets, which adds a dimension of uncertainty that is difficult to quantify. The expression "We don't know what we don't know" is more true today than ever before.

If you look beyond the noise, the panic, and the outrage, you begin to see patterns developing. Patterns that look rational and data points that I believe will bring confidence back to the markets. For example, oil prices have moved close to $50 a barrel, a three-month high. Copper continues to move higher, and the yield on the 30-year Treasury bond inches higher. All three are simple data points that by themselves seem random, but combined may suggest future economic activity. The U.S. economy is a very dynamic machine, and although it may appear as though we are frozen in time, frozen in panic, or simply discouraged, innovative people find ways to adjust to their times. I think that this rally feels different. Don't get me wrong, the headwinds to recovery are severe, but at the end of the day there are certain facts that support historical perspectives, and that is very good news...

Do I believe the American economy will survive? In the deep valley of discouragement, investors had to answer that question, as the plunging sell-off was followed by a powerful snap-back rally.

March 25, 2009

DJIA: 7,660.21
S&P: 806.29

Life Comes At You Pretty Fast

In the past week, we have once again seen government make a massive bet on re-inflating the U.S. economy. So far, the markets have responded favorably. On Monday, Treasury Secretary Timothy Geithner laid out the new toxic-assets plan, which sparked a 497-point gain in the Dow Jones average. Clearly, if you fix the banking system, housing will improve and the rest of the economy should follow. For the past few weeks we have talked about conditions being right for a market rally, and now the S&P 500 index is up more than 20% from the lows of early March. Confidence is starting to come into this market, albeit tentatively, and rightfully so, since the volatility of this market has not abated. Having said that, this rally feels different. From a technical perspective, we have had five 90% upside days out of 11. This is unprecedented and tells us that there is a shift in market psychology. As this market moves higher, money will be forced off the sidelines. (Remember, reports say that there is four times the normal amount of cash sitting there.) This rally could actually carry us to where we started this year, but probably not in a straight line.

You should also consider that this is not an environment in which the tide will take all boats up. Quality companies, those with good balance sheets, usually lead the pack. Whether this is a bear market rally or the start of a new bull market, investors need a plan of what to do next. Because as volatile as this market is, life comes at you pretty fast.

If your life circumstance has changed, talk with us about your asset allocation. Many of you know this feeling of being terrified to be in the market, yet terrified to be out. Rallies in stock prices allow you the opportunity to reduce some risk in your portfolio. Two areas worth mentioning are commodities and energy. With the Treasury printing presses going at full blast, inflation is a long-term concern, and it makes sense to start positioning your portfolio for inflationary risk.

We didn't know the strength and sustainability of the market surge from the apparent bottom. It is safe to say many investors were cautious, waiting for the next shoe to drop. With the extreme levels of volatility, the stock market resembled a casino more than the stable exchange of value we normally expect.

April 1, 2009

DJIA: 7,608.92
S&P: 797.87

Some Mud Sticks

As the saying goes, "A bull market climbs a wall of worry." Right now, that wall looks formidable. But looking beyond the current negative economic news, I'm starting to see signs of new activity and maybe, just maybe, it's not as dire as the media portray. Is there a stiff headwind to recovery? Absolutely. Will there be more disappointment along the way? I'm sure there will be. However, when the news stops getting worse, we have the environment for recovery.

The hodgepodge of public policy we have seen out of Washington has kept investors on the defensive rather than the offensive. However, there are early signs that investors are starting to look beyond the politics of the moment. With all of the new programs being initiated, it reminds me of the saying, "If you throw enough mud up on the wall, something will stick." Some of these programs will most likely stick...and work.

With massive amounts of government spending on the horizon, investors are being forced to consider that the news just might surprise on the upside. With record levels of cash on the sidelines, we have the potential for this rally continuing for a while.

We had gained more than 1,000 points on the Dow Jones index in a three-week period. This was a stunning reversal for investors, and many were on the sidelines watching. I remember wondering if we were in the eye of a financial hurricane or had we indeed seen the trough of this recession. There are still days that I wonder.

April 8, 2009

DJIA: 7,789.56
S&P: 815.55

What Flood?

Building confidence in the markets takes time, especially given the trauma of the past six months. Currently, we tend to overanalyze every piece of economic data, searching for any signs of a trend. This leaves the average investor wondering whether we are in the eye of the storm or is it truly the start of a new spring season? Of course, time will tell, but as I said two weeks ago, "at some point money will be forced off the sidelines" and a new bull market becomes obvious.

Having said that, every market has two perspectives; One is *short-term trading*, and the other is *long-term investing*. In the short term, some profit-taking seems natural, and you may want to be cautious. The market is up more than 20% in four weeks, and a little investor vertigo is normal. But the long-term trend is building the bull market case. The federal reserve is **flooding** the economy with money, trillions of dollars, in fact (that's a lot of zeroes). There is an old Wall Street saying, "Don't fight the Fed," and I see signs of the re-inflation of the U.S. economy happening. So, long-term investors may want to buy the dips. Watch commodity prices for an early indicator of future economic activity. And for now, call me a cautious bull.

April 15, 2009

DJIA: 8,029.62

S&P: 852.06

The Quiet Year

Let us start with some facts: From March 9 to April 9, the Dow Jones Industrial Average was up 23%, the S&P 500 up 26%, the NASDAQ up 30% and the Russell 2000 up 36%. This was the sharpest increase in stock prices for a 30-day period since 1933.

Now we ask a few questions. Can this performance continue? Is history the best guide as we move forward? The Panic of 2008 will be studied and analyzed for the entirety of American history. We have lived through perhaps the sharpest drop in the velocity of money, economic activity and the destructive decline of worldwide wealth in modern economic times. What's been more fascinating or disturbing, however you choose to view it, the Panic of 2008 has been covered live on worldwide news 24-7; I would say it's been the economic equivalent of "shock and awe" similar to watching the fall of Baghdad on television during the early days of Desert Storm.

Now, investors are faced with the reconstruction not only of their portfolios, but also their trust in the markets. The good news is that a financial system with high levels of economic panic and a spiraling collapse of economic activity is simply unsustainable. Once we discover what the "new normal" is for the U.S. economy, we will grow once again. Even better news, history would suggest that after a staggering blow to the economy, the economic recovery from such a massive crisis is usually stronger than normal; good news indeed.

But, trust and confidence will take time. The unprecedented government intervention and creation of money will stabilize and begin the reconstruction phase. I suspect 2009 will be viewed as the quiet year in history, while 2008 and the subsequent recovery in 2010 will be the talked-about bookends of the greatest economic event in modern times.

Investors should use this time to prepare for 2010 and beyond. You must look forward, to move beyond the panic.

April 22, 2009

DJIA: 7,969.56
S&P: 850.08

Turbulence Ahead?

This is the seventh Wednesday in a row that the markets have been higher, yet Monday's sell-off suggests that investors are not quite ready to trust the current uptrend. In fact, Monday was like hitting an air pocket while flying across the country. The drop was sudden and unexpected. When flying, the captain turns on the fasten-seatbelt sign and tells us to expect some turbulence ahead. And like passengers on a plane, investors should plan for a little turbulence over the next couple of months.

We would all like to view the markets as the glass being half-full, and after seven good weeks, it is nice to have some optimism. However, we also must keep in mind that the reconstruction process of the U.S. economy is going to be a marathon, not a sprint. Investors will need to be patient as we work our way higher over the next couple of years.

This week, I read a report by Dr. Scott Brown, the chief economist at Raymond James & Associates. He said that "recessions caused by financial crises tend to be more severe and longer-lasting." That may sound like viewing the glass as half-empty, but history has shown us that the Federal Reserve policy during financial crises tended to be overly restrictive. Perhaps Fed officials have it right this time by turning the money spigot wide open. Although in the short run a correction in stocks from overbought levels is probable, weakness in prices should be viewed as opportunities. Like the bumpy plane ride, we should focus on the destination and not worry that the plane is falling out of the sky.

Despite my own internal struggles of remaining a market participant, I was beginning to see some light at the end of the tunnel; the momentum had turned decidedly positive. As weary as most investors would be, the stress and strain of daily decisions made it difficult to enjoy the rally. I really believed the media and our political establishment would underestimate the psychological damage they had done to the investing public in March of 2009.

CHAPTER
5

April 29, 2009

DJIA: 8,016.95
S&P: 855.16

Swine Flu and Tulips

Consumer confidence was reported higher than expected on Monday. At the same time, reported cases of swine flu have been increasing. We also had the Treasury Department's bank stress test criteria released, suggesting some banks may have to raise additional capital. So what do consumer confidence, swine flu, and bank stress tests tell us? Unfortunately, very little. This is all financial noise, and it's important to sift through what are media stories and those indicators that begin to show a trend.

For example, as swine flu grabs the headlines, the 10-year Treasury bond is yielding 3% and the 30-year Treasury almost 4%. This is noteworthy for two reasons: (1.) This indicates fear is decreasing in the credit markets, and (2.) Both bond yields could be signaling inflation, suggesting that the government's attempt at re-inflating the U.S. economy may be gaining traction.

What is the trend? As I have said before, look for better news in the housing and credit markets to see an improving economy and a strengthening stock market. Those higher interest rates just may be signaling that trend. In the short run, the markets do look overbought, and after an eight-week run-up, it would be normal to see the markets pause. But with all the money on the sidelines and a lot of bad news built in, this current rally looks to have some steam behind it. Bull markets, and even bear market rallies, will climb a wall of worry, and a pattern of two steps forward and one step back would be normal.

One other little known indicator may be suggesting good times ahead. The Tulip Time Festival indicator, which looks at stock prices and tulip stems, is pointing to a higher market. (Not really, I just made that up.) But I do wish everyone a happy Tulip Festival!

May 6, 2009

DJIA: 8,410.65
S&P: 903.80

Big Ben Speaks

Federal Reserve Chairman Ben Bernanke testified to Congress yesterday and said, "We are hopeful that the very sharp decline we saw beginning last fall through early this year will moderate considerably in the near term, and we will see positive growth by the end of the year."

The glass is certainly half-full at the Federal Reserve, and I think that is the contributing factor in the rise of stock prices since the March lows. For this rally to continue, more signs of economic recovery will need to develop. It is too early to tell what the national psyche is in regard to the markets and taking risk. The high level of anxiety we experienced from the financial crisis will most likely create a cautious environment for investors for quite some time. It is reasonable to expect that as the economy starts to improve, we will continue to hear about increasing unemployment, foreclosures, and bank capital issues.

Here is the good news: I think that the stock market has priced that in already. Once again, I must mention the significant amount of cash on the sidelines. That is considerable fuel for this rally to continue, even though a pause in the short run is possible - even normal.

Of course, the big wild card is what role the government will play in moving forward. With the possibility of shifting policy coming out of Washington, investors have to remain tentative, waiting for more clarity on issues such as bank stress tests, Chrysler, and cap and trade.

May 13, 2009

DJIA: 8,469.11
S&P: 908.35

Up, Up, and... Hold on a Minute

Believe it or not, the Dow Jones and S&P 500 averages are up for the eighth straight week, but today's retail sales numbers suggests stock prices have gotten ahead of the real economy. Having said that, this week's sell-off doesn't necessarily say this current uptrend is over, but rather a well-needed rest and consolidation of gains from a spectacular rally. It is too early to tell if the past three days will be the new trend. I suspect many people have missed the early stage of this market recovery after the terrifying drop in late February, and it's nice to think that those were the bear market lows. Yet, I think we are all looking over our shoulders, wondering if the final shoe had dropped. At this point, money on the sidelines will be looking for an entry point, and that will be different for everyone.

I'm fascinated with the prices of oil and natural gas. Despite weakness in retail sales, look at energy prices. Are we seeing a repeat of last summer, when speculation pushed energy prices to triple digits for oil? It's hard not to like the energy sector and the real estate sector. I'm still looking for inflation down the road, and when you look at the commodity market and even the REIT market, I wonder if we are seeing the early signs of what is to come.

As we get through earnings season and stress tests, I think it leaves the markets in a little bit of an information void, and that should cause a little near-term weakness. However, continue to watch the financial sector for improving credit markets and employment numbers to see if the speed of shedding jobs subsides. Those would be reasons to feel a little better and actually buy stocks on weakness.

May 20, 2009

DJIA: 8,474.85

S&P: 908.13

Wake Up, Rip Van Winkle!

As of this morning, the S&P 500 is up .5% this year and the DJIA average is down 3.4% for the year, but for the 10th straight Wednesday in a row, the Dow average is higher. If you had been sleeping for the past five months and just awakened, you would look at these markets and think, "Ho-hum... Pretty boring."

We all know, however, that the past 12 months have been anything but ho-hum. In the past year, the Dow is down 33.9%; the S&P 500, 35.7%; and the NASDAQ, 30.3%. Investors today have little resemblance to investors 12 months ago, and the markets of the next few years may look completely different from the past 20.

The traumatic financial events and continued aftershocks have turned investors to move significantly toward risk aversion. The past 10 weeks have been a meteoric rise from the March lows, but momentum is slowing. The pain of sharp declines are still fresh in our minds, and only time and the building of confidence may help investors continue to push markets significantly higher.

In the short run, the markets look tired, and I would be cautious of jumping in right now. Be selective if you want to put new money to work, and look for sectors that haven't had a big run-up. This is a time to look at rebalancing and reassessing how much risk you want to take. Position yourself to respond after a possible pause in this market.

A consensus was building that the economy would eventually recover. I think it is safe to say the reality was that if the economy did not implode, it would eventually recover. However, as pertinent as that consensus was, the critical issue growing before us included the role of government in our economy.

In the midst of this crisis, the media began to embrace the economic theories of John Maynard Keynes, who advocated that free markets need the strong hand of government to balance out the basic inequities that free markets create and use monetary policy to balance the normal economic swings of an economy. One would suspect the debate over the effectiveness of Keynesian economics will only grow. What is clear to me is that, in the high anxiety of the time, thoughtful reflection on the possible unintended consequences of such government intervention in our fiscal and monetary process was not heeded and considered extreme.

The dirty little secret, of course, is that for the government to spend its resources it either must take those resources from citizens in the form of taxes or create new money, which is inflationary. But, those are details most of the media would ignore. Unfortunately, once the crisis appeared to have passed by, the focus turned to a very political and partisan agenda, creating yet another disconnect from the average citizen and investor, who understood the dire predicament the nation was falling into.

Congress and the President had underestimated the frightened and traumatized psyche of the post-crash investor. With those leaders pushing a political agenda rather than an economic agenda, they would appear to have a tin ear, as most people recognized that jobs and economic growth should be our top priorities. It is remarkable how out of touch Washington had become even as monthly employment reports continued to show a shocking deterioration of our nation's ability to create and sustain jobs.

CHAPTER

6

May 27, 2009

DJIA: 8,473.49

S&P: 910.33

One-Day Wonder!

For the past four weeks the DJIA has remained in a very narrow range. Yesterday, consumer confidence was reported to have jumped to levels of last September. This was reported as a sign of economic recovery, and the markets responded. But one-day rallies have become the norm here in the month of May. Again, I would caution investors to be selective in positioning new funds, as this market looks to be consolidating substantial gains since early March.

I find it quite interesting that six months ago, the DJIA was at 8,479. I think it reminds me of a classic bottoming process for the markets. As we know, most significant bottoms take months to form... So what will it take to move this market significantly higher? I suspect it will be better than expected corporate earnings that will be the catalyst for higher stock prices. This may seem obvious, however, in these unprecedented times, our markets and in fact the world markets have been trading on fear more than fundamentals. The market moving higher based on earnings would be a welcome sign for investors. In the short run, it was reported by JP Morgan advisors that the S&P 500 estimated PE ratio is 15 times earnings. That seems to be a reasonable PE ratio at current levels for an S&P index at 910.33.

At some point, we will start talking about 2010 and the outlook for earnings. The key component to better than expected earnings is most likely an improvement in housing. If you look at key interest rates, especially that 10-year Treasury, rising interest rates could prolong the bottoming process for housing and that would make for a subpar recovery in the economy.

June 3, 2009

DJIA: 8,740.87
S&P: 944.74

Inflation or Speculation?

The long-awaited correction for stocks continues to be, well, long-awaited. After a month of trading sideways, Monday's market broke out of that narrow range. What seemed interesting about Monday was that the announced GM bankruptcy helped push stocks up. Now we ask the questions: What does the ripple effect look like from this bankruptcy? Is the worst over, or is there another shoe to drop? (Government intervention is a growing concern.)

A positive, which could be the foundation for recovery, is the report that our nation's largest banks have raised more than $85 billion of new capital. With each day that passes, I think that there is a growing feeling that the U.S. financial system is not collapsing. As I said before, recovery in the U.S. economy would not happen until the credit and housing markets stabilize, and the credit markets are now working better... That leaves us with the housing market, which I believe will take longer. I am concerned that mortgage rates are creeping higher, and that could slow real estate sales.

What can investors do now? Review your portfolio and your risk profile. Stocks have recovered significant losses this year. Although I believe the worst is over, I also believe that having a more conservative approach to building your portfolio will allow you to better handle the changing landscape of the markets and government.

Inflation may be building into the system already... Take a look at these numbers:

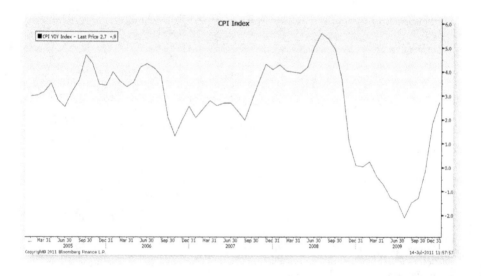

June 10, 2009

DJIA: 8,763.06
S&P: 942.43

It's the Top of the Sixth...

As we enter into the eighth quarter of general market distress, one continues to look for historical market comparisons. Is this market like that of the 1930s, 1970s, or the early 1980s? Perspective becomes challenging, as for almost two years we have analyzed unique economic data to the point of exhaustion. So, let me add to that mountain of data.

Consider this: The U.S. consumer accounts for $9.6 trillion dollars of GDP. How does that compare around the world? The entire GDP of China and India is $4.4 trillion. You would then need to throw in Great Britain and France to equal the economic force of the U.S. consumer. So where is the market heading? Look at the U.S. consumer and consider unemployment, wage growth, marginal tax rate increases, new taxes, higher energy, and interest rates. Now ask yourself if these issues are improving. Looking at these factors, I believe caution is still warranted.

I saw a baseball analogy the other day that describes our current condition well. It said, "We are still in the middle innings." As much as I would like to be in the bottom of the ninth and hit a walk-off home run, the fifth or sixth inning seems more realistic to me. The markets are trading well out in front of the economy.

June 17, 2009

DJIA: 8,504.44
S&P: 911.94

A Mountain of Cash

The dust is starting to settle in this market as we consolidate the gains from the lows in March. I believe the recovery is still out a few quarters, but the trauma of the March lows is starting to fade. As we end the second quarter, investors will be looking at corporate earnings for signs of improving business conditions. Investors should begin planning on how to commit new money to this market. The timing on this correction is hard to say, but an additional 100- to 200-point decline on the DJIA would look to be an attractive entry point back into this market. With $9 trillion on the sidelines just waiting for a pull-back in the market, we believe you do not want to be too bearish here. Corporate earnings could start showing improvement in the third quarter, and with that, expectations would surely rise for Q4 of 2009 and Q1 of 2010.

Here is something else to think about: The stimulus plan passed by Congress is slowly spilling out. It has been reported that only 7%, or $56 billion, has been spent since passage. However, of that 7%, very little has gone to job creation. With the vast majority of the government spending to come, and the mountain of cash on the sidelines, I look for a correction in this market to provide buying opportunities and probably not to be a very deep correction.

Signs are building to suggest that the recession is ending, yet they are unclear as to what the recovery will look like. Housing is really going to be the indicator to make a recovery sustainable or not.

June 24, 2009

DJIA: 8,322.91

S&P: 895.10

It's Time to Bunt

This past week, we have seen the markets weaken, as we have simply run out of steam after a very strong rally from the March lows (down roughly 6%). How deep this correction will be is difficult to say, as we are approaching corporate earnings season in July, and geopolitical events have become a wild card for broad action by Congress on many fronts.

The Federal Reserve will announce its interest rate decision this afternoon, and it is widely expected that there will be no meaningful changes... But here is what I am looking at for the next four to six weeks:

The leadership of President Obama is being put to the test by events in Iran. It is not unusual for political events to change our economic trajectory. The perception of the president's leadership will have a significant effect on Congress as members work through the wide-ranging programs that he has been pushing.

Corporate earnings and outlooks reported in July must have optimism to see a summer rally. As an investor looking at the next couple of months, I would suggest thinking in baseball terms. Sometimes, you simply bunt to put your team in scoring position.

We are in a correction, so caution is still warranted, but we also believe it is a mistake to become too bearish, with significant developments unfolding in July and August. Rarely does the market know what triggers the next move, but who would have guessed that Twitter™ could bring regime change in Iran.

We were coming to the end of May, and all seemed quiet – almost too quiet, in fact. If it is possible for a nation to experience post-traumatic stress syndrome, then I believe in the relative calm that we were experiencing, the nation was provided a reflective moment, allowing thoughtful appreciation for the economic near-death experience we had come through.

I remember my mind drifting toward historic reflection and that it would take a generation to put this experience behind us. I tried to imagine the hard times of the Great Depression and wondered what similarities there must be.

"Complacency" was a word I kept thinking about as the desperate attempts to rebuild our economy were unfolding. From the rubble of bankruptcies and sudden reversals, investors were being given a historic opportunity to put capital to work. The problem, of course, was we were all weary; weary of loss, weary of uncertainty, and weary of simply being lost in transition as our economy experienced massive dislocations.

In the early months of the recovery, it was if we were being asked to decipher a riddle of seemingly disconnected events, but for the weary, riddles are hard to comprehend, let alone solve.

Monday, June 8, 2009, General Motors was removed from the Dow Jones Industrial Average. It would be replaced by Cisco Systems. In this deep well of economic destruction, you find moments that simply take your breath. General Motors would be just one of many corporate giants to fall victim to the financial crisis, yet this company represented more of what we lost than the simple balance-sheet companies that crumpled like paper in that season.

To my mind, General Motors falling into Chapter 11 became a symbolic act. The old axiom "As General Motors goes, so goes the nation" was echoing in my mind, providing a Dantésque picture of what America had become. It was like having your grandfather pass away. General Motors was our nation's corporate patriarch – a patriarch with faults, but revered nonetheless for the formidable presence it once commanded as the titan of industry. No matter how you felt about the bankruptcy, it just seemed appropriate and respectful to grieve.

CHAPTER

7

July 1, 2009

Third-Quarter Surprise?

The second quarter ended yesterday with a whimper, although I believe we have clear signs that the economy is bottoming. It is not clear if a sustainable recovery will occur this year. Yesterday, a surprise decline in consumer confidence dampened investors' enthusiasm for a strong summer rally. I think the magnitude of government involvement in the economy and the realization that government intervention is much more than "crisis management" is starting to weigh heavily on investors' outlooks as the consequences of potential new policies are simply unknown. Markets do not like uncertainty, and I would expect some volatility over the next few months as Congress attempts to push forward with major initiatives.

For the S&P 500 the second quarter did finish up 11%, and this is the first positive quarter in more than a year. What is most important to note as we end the second quarter is that the markets have moved beyond crisis mode, and we are looking forward to corporate earnings being released over the next six weeks. If earnings are better than expected, you could see employment numbers improve, and a late-summer rally could be possible. Until we see better earnings, I remain cautious and expect a range-bound market.

As I reflect back, it's still unclear when the role of government moved from crisis management to the sense that the size and scope of government was actually too small and should play a more sub-stantial role. Had we really become the ancient Roman Empire, col-lapsing under the weight of our own largesse? Would we begin a long decline, a trajectory no longer ascending, but rather descending, shooting toward the rising sun of the East? My sense is that the role of China remains unclear – unclear whether it's our savior or our ruin, like the financial barbarians from the East waiting to plunder our Rome.

July 8, 2009

Keep Your Powder Dry!

The markets closed at a two-month low and it is looking as if we will head lower. With the lack of economic fundamentals supporting stock prices, you will see momentum shifts, which tend to get extended up and down. The fundamentals we do have continue to be weak, especially employment. The bond market strength over the past two weeks tells me it will be a difficult summer for stocks. Falling interest rates tend to be a barometer of economic activity. This may be good for borrowers, as mortgage rates could head lower.

Corporate earnings season begins today, with Alcoa reporting after the market closes. Any hope of reversing this correction would have to be earnings coming in much better than expected, but I doubt we will see that until the third- or fourth-quarter earnings come out. We simply need more evidence that the economic recovery is possible than what we are presently seeing. The talk in Washington of a second stimulus bill is dampening investor confidence, and at the end of the day, I would be strongly cautious. Keep an eye on commodity prices... My hunch is that commodity prices will lead the next rally, if we do, in fact, see one.

We seem stuck between a current deflationary environment and the prospects of an inflationary environment. Consumers are finding incentives to save money and pay down debt, which creates a stalemate of current realities and future expectations. We all want the economy to improve, but it will be time, not Washington, that brings that about.

July 22, 2009

Breaking Through the Ceiling?

As we make our way through corporate earnings season, the markets have been cheering as earnings on balance have been coming in above expectations. This news has pushed stock prices to the high end of a trading range that peaked in early June. Two weeks ago, I mentioned watching commodity prices to signal a market rally. Copper, gold, oil and natural gas all have jumped, which could be signaling some strength in the economy. The question now, of course, is will the party continue? Will stock prices break through the ceiling of the June highs, and start a new leg up in this market?

It would surprise me to see this market have a significant breakthrough based on the data we are seeing today. Yes, the U.S. economy is healing, but bad news not getting worse is hardly the economic foundation we will need to have a full-blown bull market. However, I would also say that now is not a time to become too gloomy. A new bull market will need to climb a formidable wall of worry, but the economic innovations and management skills of U.S. corporations should start to materialize and help to bring confidence back.

We are looking at a multi-year recovery in the U.S. economy, and quick fixes or a quick recovery is most likely not in the cards. We are in a period where dividends on stocks and interest on bonds will be a major piece of your total return. It takes patience to traverse this investment landscape. A well-rounded portfolio may have to be more diversified than in years past, and should be flexible enough to make strategic changes as the economy goes from the current deflation we are experiencing to the inflation scenario that seems to be on our horizon. We continue to search for companies and opportunities that we believe could be long-term survivors on the other side of recovery.

July 29, 2009   DJIA: 9,096.72

S&P: 979.62

Did I Say Powder Keg?

In the past two weeks, what could have gone right, has. Corporate earnings have been solid, with a surprising 75% of corporations reporting and beating expectations. We have avoided a spike in energy prices over this summer, which was a massive tax on consumers a year ago, and the very aggressive Obama agenda has begun to frazzle and lose momentum. Like I said...what could have gone right, has.

As I mentioned last week, I believe it's a mistake to be too gloomy, and likewise, a mistake to throw caution to the wind and believe the "all clear" flag is waving. Four short months ago, the unthinkable was happening. The U.S. economy was close to collapse, and the banking system was teetering toward nationalization. A thin layer of confidence covers this market, and this economic recovery is still fragile. But there is a powder keg of cash sitting on the sidelines, and as we feel more confident, we tend to take more risk. This powder keg of cash is getting anxious. I believe this anxiety of holding cash has the potential of putting a floor on any correction, and could extend the current rally. At the end of the day, we still need to ask: Are the current earnings reports sufficient to sustain a significant rally from this point?

We do know that earnings reports are winding down, and as we roll into August and September, a void of earnings news will focus investors on something else. Most likely, we will focus on the economy and employment. This makes me nervous, however, I would use a correction in stock prices as an opportunity to accumulate quality investments. What is feeling better is that as a nation, we seem to have steadied ourselves. Confidence will grow from this, and, hopefully, we should not need to fear while looking into the future and 2010. My experience tells me that when confidence returns, there will be a sense, as investors, that we need to play catch up. This results in taking more risk than we need to, and simply adds to our discomfort. Patience and strategy can help to rebuild your portfolio and move you closer to your ultimate objectives. Too much risk is difficult to see until after the fact... Slow and steady may sound cliché, but it has stood the test of time.

August 5, 2009

How's the Weather?

The two worst times in the market happen when: (1.) You are in the market and it crashes, or (2.) Being in cash when the market melts up which is an odd way to describe unrelenting upward pressure for stocks. In seven months, investors have experienced the trauma of a meltdown, and watched twice as the market melted up. The fear of losing and the fear of missing out are powerful negative forces in being a successful long-term investor. What I find interesting is the fact that this is happening during a period of history in which the American culture is at some type of inflection point not seen since the late 1960s. If the last 18 months had not been so painful, it truly would be fascinating to see a new era in history born.

For today, I think back to the phrase Alan Greenspan used in the late 1990s, "irrational exuberance." Clearly, all the cash on the sidelines is in motion, and like musical chairs, there is a scramble for the last chair. In the short run, this makes me nervous. The average investor should look forward and make decisions on what's ahead, rather than focus on what was lost, or what you missed out on. Melt ups, like meltdowns, can be and usually are irrational. In the past 17 trading days, we have seen the Dow Jones average rise more than 1,200 points. The question you must ask is whether this summer rally is based on strong fundamentals and an improving economy, or simply cash flooding into the market not wanting to miss out.

The outlook and sentiment have certainly shifted, and I believe a normal correction will be used by investors to buy the market. So be cautious in the near term, but look to put cash to work on weakness in stocks. As I said last week, this is not a time to be too gloomy. The markets can be a good barometer of what is to come for the U.S. economy, and the weather may just be clearing.

Quietly, the third quarter of 2009 unleashed a barrage of positive corporate earnings reports that surprised many of us. Something had changed, and as if a switch flipped on, corporate America began to show stunning resilience. One company after another would announce better than expected results and talk of the future in terms of optimism, albeit guarded – but upbeat just the same.

A summer rally was brewing like the giant thunderclouds of July. At the same time, Congress was recessed, but home for the holidays.

Town hall meetings were being held, and the discontent of voters was causing turmoil for elected officials who were confident the current health care proposal would be welcomed. The outpouring of concern and criticism represented the pent-up frustration most people were experiencing; not just for health care, but also the months of loss most had experienced.

The unemployment rate was rising to 9.5% – and we know now, it would head even higher. The mood of voters was angry, yet the mood of investors was something different all together.

It was fascinating, on the one hand, to witness average citizens rise in true democratic protest, while observing the power of contrarian thinking as billions of dollars would leave the sidelines and began buying common stocks. The summer of 2009 presented us with two major events: first, the bull market for stocks would have sustaining power, and, second, at town halls around the country, the Tea Party movement was being born.

I flashed back to the numerous town hall meetings I attended with Congressman and Michigan gubernatorial candidate, Pete Hoekstra. In Standish, Michigan, we participated in a town hall in a community where, as you may remember, President Obama had suggested moving Guantanamo Bay prisoners to a state penitentiary that was being closed. Traveling the state, we had the opportunity to participate in a number of health care town hall meetings. I remember thinking this would be historic; so many people, of all political backgrounds having their chance simply to be heard. My hope for America was alive in those meetings; they were inspiring, representing the best of our democracy!

CHAPTER
8

August 12, 2009

DJIA: 9,241.45

S&P: 994.35

Too Much of a Good Thing?

After a spectacular summer rally, I think it may be time to get out of the pool for a while. The market seems to be at over-bought levels, and a short-term correction would certainly be a normal reaction to this kind of run-up. Does it always happen? Well, not always. In fact, as I write this, the Dow Jones average is up triple digits, erasing yesterday's decline. But it's rare to not see some consolidation of gains after a substantial rise in stock prices. Later today the Federal Reserve will announce its decision on short-term interest rates. It is expected to make no changes, but we will listen carefully to any subtle changes in its policy statement. Obviously, interest rates by the Federal Reserve won't stay at near-zero forever.

The real question as we finish reviewing second-quarter corporate earnings is whether the third quarter will be a continuation of better than expected earnings, or did cost cutting give us the good numbers, and won't be repeated in the third quarter. One quarter doesn't make a trend. I suspect that investors will be cautious for a while. But if we get early signs of a strong third quarter, cash could certainly flood into the markets, cutting short any correction. In the meantime, put your playbook together. With cash on the sidelines, use this time to plan where you want to put it. Look at your allocations, and simply be prepared for a pull-back in prices and take advantage of it. We really believe that this market has forced investors to be more tactical in their portfolios, and one simple strategy is to harvest some gains. You can do that by dollar-cost-averaging out of the market. An all-or-nothing strategy does not seem appropriate in such a fast-moving market, but balancing does seem appropriate. In the next six weeks we will see a slowdown in corporate news. Politics and economic news will take the headlines. That tends to give us some volatility, so don't be surprised. Just be prepared for a better year-end.

August 19, 2009   DJIA: 9,217.94
                                          S&P: 989.67

It Takes an Air Traffic Controller

Although the markets are trading closely to where they were last week, it certainly feels different, as investor sentiment has turned cautious. The idea of a sharp V-shaped recovery is fading as the strength of the U.S. consumer is recovering more slowly than hoped. In fact, we have seen a real increase in consumer savings, not consumer spending. What did catch my eye this week was a fairly sharp decline in interest rates. I believe that the drop in rates and rally in bonds confirm the notion that economic activity is falling short of expectations, and pushing off the inflation fear that is growing in the marketplace.

I still believe that short-term caution is the correct stance, and it is not too late to take some profit and keep some cash available to buy this market on weakness. I think that the third-quarter earnings reports in October will be the next best chance for a good rally. Special situations will always be the case, even in a market that is in correction mode. For example, news hit yesterday of a 20-year deal between Exxon Mobil (XOM) and PetroChina (PTR) for a long-term supply of liquefied natural gas. This may be starting a trend of countries looking to ensure long-term energy needs for an improving worldwide economy. I think that deals like the one reported are a good sign for economic recovery in 2010 and beyond. (Check www.zccapital.com for up-to-date research on the energy sector.)

The wild card is Washington, and what legislation, if any, Congress passes and the President signs into law. Perhaps nothing will happen, and legislation will simply fade or morph into something else. An interesting thought would be if the President changes course and alters the bloated stimulus bill passed in February. That is the type of event that can be a catalyst to renewed optimism. The markets, by and large, have the known news built in; it is the surprises that cause real price movements. I always wonder,what is not on my radar that should be?

August 26, 2009

DJIA: 9,539.29

S&P: 1,028.00

Cash, Cash Everywhere!

At the beginning of August, we talked about a possible melt up for the markets, as cash on the sidelines gets "anxious" and moves into the market in an attempt to not miss out. I want to revisit some of the recent data I have seen to put this in perspective. According to a report from Wood Asset Management, as of July 31, 2009, you could purchase every share of the S&P 500 for $8,659 trillion. Currently, the amount sitting in a cash position is $9,540 trillion. In other words, there is still plenty of cash to keep the current trend and momentum moving.

However, when I look at valuations and technical indicators on this market, the picture is one of a very extended rally and a market statistically overbought. As oversold as the market was in March, statistically it is now overbought at similar levels. According to Dorsey Wright and Associates, this market is more than 86% overbought. Clearly, in the short run, I caution you to watch your step. Sometimes, return of principal is a better objective than return on principal, and this feels like one of those times.

Does the market need to drop from these levels? Well, in most cases, a correction after a significant advance would be normal. Having said that, times have been anything but normal for the past 12 months. It is possible that the excesses in this market will be corrected by a range-bound market that simply moves sideways as the economy improves and corporate profits move higher. For now, accumulate some cash, take a few profits, and wait for a better risk vs. reward scenario to present itself. Buying this market on weakness seems to be appropriate.

September 2, 2009   DJIA: 9,310.60

                                         S&P: 998.04

Let the Games Begin

After a great summer rally, you can just feel the momentum swing away from the market. Not only have we seen stocks start to stall out, but a quick look at the selected commodities in this report show a similar pattern. Is this the correction many have expected? My near-term caution on the market is based on my sense that the month of September will be a difficult one for the markets to make progress. I do believe a correction is in the mix, and yesterday's sell-off suggests that volatility is increasing.

This may, in fact, be the beginning of a correction, but don't despair over it. I believe any weakness in this market allows for a gradual reallocation of your portfolio. For those of you with cash on the sidelines, use weakness to add to or initiate new stock holdings. In any market correction, certain sectors will be harder hit than others. Look for opportunity in high-quality stocks or mutual funds that correct more than the overall market, and be patient. History would tell us that a correction could last four to six weeks or longer. Pick your own price point where you want to buy and let the market come to you.

One last point. I hate to bring up politics, but Congress will be back in session next week, and if the month of August showed us anything, it was that there is deep contention in terms of major legislation proposed. I don't know what will happen in Congress, but I do know that politics can cause anxiety and uncertainty in the markets. September will set the pace for the balance of the year, and I think that investors will watch carefully to see what legislation will mean to them, and the ultimate prospects for passing broad and far-reaching programs. We don't know who the winners and losers will be in this process. I do believe, however, that investors will eventually figure that out and take action to capitalize on the changes. At the end of the day, this is one more factor that leads me to believe September will be difficult.

Relatively speaking, the markets had performed quite well from the March lows, yet, emotionally, I don't believe we were ready to look forward. *I feel as though I'm living far away; I wandered off, and would like to find my way home.* Sometimes, my personal journal captures the sentiment of the times well. This sentence I jotted down was the look I saw on the faces of many investors and many looking for jobs.

The America we had been living in had been replaced by an unfamiliar land. Being a stranger in a far-off land makes you tentative, reluctant to embrace what you see in front of your eyes. I believe investors were viewing the markets like an unfamiliar land, one too treacherous to trust, and too volatile to embrace. Once again, that phrase was creeping into my conversations, "If I had only known," but this time people were afraid of being left behind this growing rally.

With the strength in corporate profits, for the first time since the crisis began, I began to wonder about the possibility of seeing the Dow Jones index pierce the 10,000 level. The Federal Reserve was remaining accommodative, in terms of monetary policy keeping interest rates near zero, and that gave me reason to believe unproductive and low-yielding cash would enter the markets. Re-inflating the U.S. economy would become a "grand experiment," an experiment that to date has no conclusion.

We were coming up on the one year anniversary of the collapse of Lehman Brothers. The echoes of such an abrupt and colossal failure would continue to haunt the recovery, creating moments of anxiety that in turn created more volatility.

CHAPTER
9

September 9, 2009   DJIA: 9,497.34
                                                    S&P: 1,025.39

Glittering Gold

A good weatherman knows his barometer. This gauge
helps determine a change in the weather. Some
might say that, for the investor, gold is a good
barometer. With the price of gold at $1,000 per
ounce, is this predictive or simply speculation?
Also notable is the fact that copper is up 55% in
the past four months. As an investor, you are
always looking for clues as to a developing trend.
Gold prices rising, copper prices rising, and a
falling dollar are three things I'm curious about.
Is this inflation or just an improving economy?

Well, at some point, federal deficits have consequences. Last week the Office of Management and
Budget projected $9 trillion in cumulative deficits
over the next 10 years. Some have suggested this
number is low and could reach $12 trillion. These
are sobering numbers that have consequences. The
speed at which the debt is accumulating is stunning.
Consider this fact: One year ago, the Bush administration and the Office of Management and Budget
reported that by 2012 the federal budget would be
in surplus. The debt would be estimated to be 36%
of GDP. What a stark contrast 12 months has brought
us. The federal budget deficit will reach more than

70% of GDP in the next 12 months and will continue to rise. Deficits certainly have consequences.

My point this morning is that although inflation is not a problem today, clearly there is an undertone of anxiousness about inflationary pressures building as the economy improves or government expands. Tonight, the President will make a speech to a joint session of Congress. By all measures, this is a critical, perhaps even a defining, moment for the President and the nation. The trajectory of government spending and deficits is what the markets will focus on. Inflation could be a consequence of expanding deficits. Our markets are quite resilient, and the past 12 months have shown that. The good news is that we can make adjustments to take advantage of the changing economic conditions. Despite all of the drama, there is usually a little nugget of gold somewhere. As my football coach used to say, "Be patient, and let the play develop." That's good advice for all investors.

September 16, 2009

DJIA: 9,683.41
S&P: 1,052.63

Bernanke: "The recession is over!"

One year ago, the Dow Jones fell more than 500 points. Lehman Brothers, Merrill Lynch and AIG, stalwarts of the financial system, collapsed. So, what have we learned? A year ago I said, *"This is a treacherous short-term market and we simply do not know the interconnectedness of these financial events."* We now know, like a house of cards, that it is all connected, and we struggle to find the appropriate public policy responses to prevent this from happening again. I believe we still don't fully understand the connectedness of the new financial paradigm.

Having said all of that, the trauma of the past 12 months is subsiding and the economy is starting to show signs of healing. The markets continue to surge higher as all the cash we have talked about is finding its way into stocks. The correction, which many (myself included) believe is just around the corner, has yet to materialize. For the moment, there is solid momentum to push toward a 10,000 DJIA. I remain cautious with a positive bias. Corporate earnings will start to be announced in four weeks, and unlike July, I wonder if our expectations will be too high, rather than too low.

So what does history say about a time such as this? As I said one year ago, three pillars of finance collapsed, and the public attitude was that we were headed for a new Great Depression. I don't know how history will write this era, but I do believe that we all have reached our own conclusions. Today we are grappling with philosophical issues. As a nation, will our attitude be that capitalism is somehow defective and government is more efficient? Or, will we believe government is the root cause of the credit collapse, and it was government that failed us, not the free markets? We have been here before, the years 1933 and 1977 come to mind. In fact, President Jimmy Carter proposed national health care in 1977. The good news is that patient investors were rewarded, and despite our cultural divide, the American people have always found a way to prosper. After all, the recession is officially over.

September 23, 2009

DJIA: 9,829.87

S&P: 1,071.66

If the Shoe Fits

Waiting for the next shoe to drop has been the overall attitude of many market participants. In fact, take away the anxiousness of the times and you would have a good old fashioned bull market on your hands. Perspective is everything, but how we see this market is most likely tied to how confident you are and feel. Today the Federal Reserve will conclude its two-day meeting, and, without a doubt, the vast majority of economists expect the Fed to make no changes to interest rates. Time will tell if rates near zero can re-inflate this economy.

With attention focused on Washington, it seems as though the markets have focused more on a possible global recovery in early 2010 rather than getting caught up in the daily drama of politics. Cash on the sidelines has trickled in, and without a catalyst of the negative kind, money will continue to move into this market. In fact, as of this morning, the DJIA is up 50% from the lows of March. Although a correction of 5% to 10% would seem normal, it just doesn't feel as if it is normal right now. Perhaps this market is signaling better days ahead, but it is difficult to see in the short run where the optimism is coming from to sustain this current rally.

However, it seems reasonable to me to buy on any pull-back in this market. It would be unusual, very unusual, not to see some consolidation of gains. (Take advantage of that.) Also, keep an eye on Washington. If the Senate, in dealing with health care, should use the procedure known as reconciliation, whereby legislation can pass with a 51-vote majority, this would require a recalibration in my mind as to what stocks are worth in a world where a 51-vote majority rules. I would suggest that a tremendous amount of uncertainty would come into the market, and that long-awaited correction could happen. But the shoe hasn't dropped, and for the moment, investors are willing to take on more risk for higher returns... And that really is a bull market.

September 30, 2009   DJIA: 9,742.20
                                      S&P: 1,060.61

Halloween?

Today will end the third quarter of 2009, and what
a quarter it has been. Indications show that the
S&P 500 index is up more than 15% for the quarter,
which is the best quarterly performance since 1998.
After a disastrous start to 2009, the index stands
up 16.71% heading into this final day. The financial
earthquake that stunned the U.S. economy late last
year and early this year has had severe consequences
that still are unfolding. As you know, aftershocks
are a natural result of an earthquake, and with
our economic earthquake this should happen, too.
What's important to remember is that aftershocks
are normal and should be expected. Although the
worst of the crisis may be behind us, this is no
time to be complacent as an investor. As we begin
the fourth quarter, we know October has been a
month of historical difficulties for the financial
markets, and after a strong third quarter, I look
for the start of October to be hit with headwinds
that could lead to the correction many expect. In
other words, Halloween may come on October 1st,
rather than the 31st, for investors.

Consider this: The 30-year Treasury bond is yielding 4.03%, the lowest level since last April. Copper prices have declined 10% in the past month. Consumer confidence unexpectedly fell in September, and mortgage demand fell, despite lower rates. These are deflationary indicators consistent with a slowing economy. Does that mean the rally for stocks is over? I don't know. However, you can feel the headwinds, and if we are going to have gains, it won't be a gentle ride higher.

One gauge I must mention is a contrarian indicator. Investors throughout August have deposited $209 billion into bond mutual funds, compared with just $15.2 billion for stock funds. In other words, 93 cents of every investable dollar is going into bonds, not stocks, and yet the market has climbed 15% for the quarter. The reason I point this out is that normally the average investor is wrong. I guess this is why I may be cautious in the very near term, but optimistic for the long run. So be patient and take advantage of what this markets presents us. Continue to be ready to buy on weakness.

I'm always fascinated with headlines. Good ones tell a story; others foreshadow events to come. In September of 2009, two headlines from the Wall Street Journal fell into the latter category: "Muammar Gaddafi Celebrates Forty Years in Power" and "Oil Discovery Highlights BP's Resurgence." Perhaps in normal times we would have given these stories more thought or more reflection, but in the confusion of crisis economics, we tend to focus on the here and now, letting questions of consequences pass on by. I have to wonder, is there a headline today that's foretelling 2012?

When a psychological barrier is breached, you take notice. Gold prices pushing through $1,000 per ounce seemed to shock investors and for at least the moment made us pause — not for a dictator celebrating 40 years of rule, and not for an oil company celebrating a new-found oil field in the Gulf of Mexico, but the price of an ounce of yellow metal.

But, why — what was happening to push gold to such prices? Was this just one more bubble waiting to burst? In a skittish market, investor paranoia can create havoc, and nothing creates more conspiracy theories than the price of gold. It wasn't just the price of gold moving higher, but commodities across the board surging, signaling economic activity to come.

Signs of sustainable economic growth would begin to form a trend, a trend that started with the reported second-quarter earnings and continued with the anticipation of earnings for the third quarter to be released in October. Despite the Washington noise on health care, investors seemed to be looking forward into 2010 and anticipating better news.

I believe that, as a nation, we were cautiously optimistic — perhaps confused and surely concerned, but in any case, at last looking forward. History has shown me that investors can make money with a big government or a small government.

The second part of that truth is uncertainty over what the size will be. That tends to be more difficult to deal with. With Congress going back into session, the size and scope of government began creating a fog of uncertainty that may take years to clear away.

CHAPTER
10

October 7, 2009

DJIA: 9,731.25
S&P: 1,054.72

Curve Ahead

After a quick 5% correction to begin the month of October, the markets turned positive, looking forward to the release of third-quarter earnings. Earnings season begins this week as Alcoa announces its third-quarter results. Back in July, second-quarter earnings surprised on the upside, and the markets have rallied ever since. Another earnings season above expectations could be the catalyst that confirms an economic recovery and pushes the markets to new 52-week highs, despite the significant wall of worry that many investors feel.

My own wall of worry has a foundation built on the unknown. I simply don't know what I don't know, much like driving in a thick fog. In a fog, you hope that you know where the road is going, and as long as the road is straight, you can make good progress. However, the unseen curves present the problem.

When it comes to the economy, there are signs of improvement, but sustainable improvements are the real worry. In my view, the U.S. economy is teetering between a second recession and a recovery with high inflation that has not been seen in 30 years. Investors should understand that a case can be made for either scenario, and diversification is key to weathering this period of time and a foggy outlook. Unfortunately, in the world of economics and investing, there will not be a sign that says "Caution: Curve Ahead."

October 14, 2009

DJIA: 9,871.06
S&P: 1,073.19

Reluctant Bull

When I try to build the case for a new bull market, I seem to get lost in the hundreds of thousands of jobs still being lost. Likewise, as I try to build the case for a second part of the recession and a renewed bear market, I seem to get lost in the trillions of dollars waiting to become productive. Economists debate back and forth at the direction of the markets and the U.S. economy. What we have is a market that is struggling to break the 10,000 level, yet perseveres the selling pressure of profit-taking. Since mid July, the Dow Jones averages have traded between 9,000 and where we are today (9,900). This recession may be over, but it seems to have a long tail, and many investors have long memories. As we bracket this range in the market, it is very difficult to fully embrace a new bull market. But with Intel's earnings release and solid momentum behind the technology sector, it is just a matter of time before the artificial ceiling of 10,000 is broken.

I don't believe that third-quarter corporate profits will be the all-clear sign for the markets. What I do believe is that, come November, after many companies have reported earnings, it will be confirmed that the current level of stock prices are fair, and we can focus on 2010 and beyond. Back in February and March, many were not sure there would be much of a future, and certainly could not picture what 2010 would look like. In other words, we now know our new normal, and it is OK.

The good news is that like an unwelcomed guest, this recession will someday leave and we can move on and move forward. I think it is good that despite the hardship still present that is reported in our daily newspapers, the American people are moving forward. You can hear it in their voices and you can see it clearly in the markets. The stock market is a very good barometer of confidence, and when you look at the market, there seems to be a strength in this rally. This confidence may sustain the optimism until we see the clear signs of an economic recovery and an improving job market.

The bottom line is that despite unemployment, housing and Washington politics, the American investor is back. The question now is this: Is the American consumer back? A good Christmas season is probably all we need for a roaring bull market. Certainly, setbacks are possible and probable, but don't be afraid to reengage this market, especially on any weakness.

October 21, 2009

DJIA: 10,041.48
S&P: 1,091.06

The Tide Is In

My confidence in the prospects of the U.S. economy and our financial markets lies squarely on my belief in the American people. We sometimes lose sight of why millions of people come to America both legally and illegally to build a better life for themselves and their loved ones. The entrepreneurial spirit is a powerful force. Therefore, despite the interference of outside forces or our own government, the financial system of the United States will right itself and forge new beginnings for millions of Americans. A broad perspective on our economy helps us look at the day-to-day distractions as problems to solve, rather than reasons to quit.

Having said that, the day-to-day distractions can certainly make you wonder where this market is heading in the short run. The signs of recovery are certainly beginning to show. The stock market since early March has been forecasting a recovery of some kind, and I think you could say that "the tide took all boats up." So what about the fourth quarter? Here is a quote from Wood Asset Management that sums it all up fairly well: "Given the stabilization in financial markets, accommodative monetary policy and improvements in key economic indicators in the critical areas of housing and industrial production, we continue to believe that sectors with pro-cyclical characteristics, such as technology, energy, materials and global indust-rials will outperform."

Well, the tide is in, and the fourth quarter should give us a stock picker's market, as the unintended consequences of massive government intervention will start to show, and most likely will lead us to a shallow recovery. There should be enough growth for inflation to become a real concern. However, until the Federal Reserve tightens monetary policy, the themes that led the third quarter should continue to lead the fourth. I'm still a buyer of stocks on weakness, especially in those areas mentioned above.

October 28, 2009

DJIA: 9,882.17

S&P: 1,063.41

Two Times
_____

I began my career in 1982, when unemployment was peaking at 10.8% and the U.S. economy was dealing with the worst inflation we had ever experienced. The wall of worry investors were presented with was formidable. We know today that the seeds of the greatest bull market in our nation's history were sown in the 1981-1982 time period. Herein lies the question of whether we are sowing the seeds of a new period of prosperity in the midst of this current recession. In 10 years, will we reflect back at this time and know it was a great time to invest in the U.S. economy? With a growing divide of philosophy and opinion, the American people are more anxious and frustrated than optimistic, or dare I say, hopeful. I think it is safe to say we face a formidable wall of worry.

I find comfort in knowing that history has much to say if we will only listen. Great divides are not new. America has had its share of growing pains. Yet some divides become defining moments and seem to change the trajectory of a nation. The Civil War was fought over a deep divide of cultural values. Likewise, the Vietnam War divided our culture and ushered in the emergence of the baby boomer generation. Two times in history, two times of deep cultural divides, and two times our economy recovered. I'm not sure how history will describe our current divide. Only time will tell if there will be a defining moment unfolding from the Great Recession of 2008-2009.

It is always difficult to see, but opportunity tends to be a byproduct of uncertain times. I don't want to minimize the pain and personal angst difficult times create, but from the narrow view of investing, there simply will be opportunities. I have said this before, and I will say it again: I remain short-term cautious, but long-term hopeful. This market seems to be finding a range, a range that could last for several months. Now is the time to reassess your risk profile and outlook. If you believe that inflation is your greatest risk, start moving assets into those investments that outperform with inflation. If you believe the economy is heading toward continued deflation, then plan for that and move to preserve capital. The best time to think and plan is when there is a lull in the action, and I think we may have a few months to do that.

November 4, 2009

DJIA: 9,771.91
S&P: 1,045.41

Middle Ground

You don't have to look too far to realize the current market is in a period of consolidation. The run-up in stock prices helped erase the deep sell-off in most stocks around the world, and now many of the technical indicators I follow are registering a correction. The hardest hit has been the NASDAQ, as many technology stocks have pulled off their highs. But don't get too pessimistic. It has been reported that more than 80% of companies reporting earnings are forecasting better outlooks, and it's been a while since we have heard news like that. Certainly it seems as though the tenor of our investment dialogue is more positive.

Despite better forecasts, it has also been reported that money moving into bond funds is still running at record rates. The money that flows into equity funds is still just a trickle. Here is something to think about: There is as much money going into bond funds today as there was money going into stock funds in 1999, the height of the technology bubble. Does this tell us anything? The contrarian in me wants to buy stocks. When the investing herd is moving in one direction, many times the opportunity is where you are not looking. Yesterday, Warren Buffet bought the remainder of Burlington Northern

Railroad for $26 billion. A railroad needs a better economy to thrive, and $26 billion is a lot of money, even for Warren Buffet.

On the political front, the U.S. economy tends to perform well for a country governed from the political middle. Last nights' gubernatorial elections in Virginia and New Jersey may be signaling the end of a rapid political slide to the far left. Some will say that is good, others will say that is bad (we are a deeply divided nation). But either way, I think the financial markets will welcome this development and the hope of some political balance. It is from this middle ground that Americans will be less disheartened, less anxious, and more confident about their future. As I have said before, the best barometer of confidence in America is the U.S. stock market. I would not be afraid to buy stocks on near-term weakness.

November 11, 2009

DJIA: 10,246.97
S&P: 1,093.01

Money, Money Everywhere

The U.S. central bank holds 286,900,700.71 ounces of gold. Yesterday, gold closed at $1,105 per ounce. Some have said with the impending inflation on horizon, gold could climb above $2,000 per ounce. Do the math, and I think you would agree that's a lot of gold. But what about the rest of the world? Certainly we transferred our national wealth offshore, right? Well, China, Japan, Russia, India and the U.K. combined have 3,054 metric tons of gold. That is not even half of the 8,133.5 metric tons that the U.S. holds. What I'm trying to say is that the "death spiral" of debt that the media would have you believe exists may, in fact, be over-stated. The U.S. economy is still the largest and strongest economy in the world.

This perspective on gold reserves does not minimize the economic climate and difficulties we face today. With 10.2% unemployment and higher inflation expected in the future, we have plenty to worry about. But this stock market has been quite resilient to all of the anxiety the American people are feeling. I know gold reserves as one data point does not suggest a trend or ring the all-clear bell. I point this out because sometimes we just lose perspective. The media today work hard at providing 24-7 financial news coverage, and I would suggest that the vast majority of news is simply looking in the rear-view mirror and rarely predictive of our future.

I believe that we are in a market correction, and it seems quite normal to me. The Federal Reserve is keeping interest rates at near-zero, and has said it will keep them there for some time. Now, you may not like the heavy hand of government as we are seeing it play out over the course of this recession, but with the Federal Reserve pumping cash out like Monopoly money, it is hard for me to not see stocks higher in the next few quarters. Supply and demand suggests that if there is more money chasing a fixed amount of assets, those assets tend to rise in price. Sometimes this complex financial world is just that simple. I think you should buy stocks on weakness, or at least until the Fed changes course.

We seemed to be settling in, finding a new rhythm to our day-to-day lives after a tumultuous spring. The news was dominated by stories of health care proposals, and the deep divide of political and philosophical issues was never more apparent. In some ways, this was an amazing magic act, a sleight-of-hand directing our attention toward Washington, while the economy continued to build momentum from the sharp and sudden recession the financial crisis caused.

Just recently, we experienced a dire prediction by Harold Camping of Family Radio, who claimed to know the Biblical end times, the rapture, was supposed to occur May 21, 2011—it didn't. I allude to this simply to describe how people felt about the market's strong performance heading into the fourth quarter. Many investors remained on the sidelines, feeling cursed by God; they bought when they should have sold and sold when they should have bought. Sometimes, that sense of missing out is as powerful as losing all together.

As an investor, you just want to keep moving. Being on the wrong side of the markets will leave you often paralyzed and unable to keep up with a world spinning too fast.

For myself, I could see positive signs developing, yet I still had this sense of meandering, not sure of my ultimate destination; when my soul wanders I turn inward, reflecting on the whys. Why is this happening? Why is this happening to me? Why can't I control the anxiousness I feel? In this case, "why" was a cousin to "if I had only known." "Grieving" was a good word to describe the national mood.

The "new normal" was a phrase bouncing around to describe our current state of affairs; but frankly, I wasn't ready to accept that. I wanted "my America" back, the country that had optimism built into its DNA and had answers to the world's complex problems. Deep down, I know we all had a unique version of "our America," but I think it's been a while since the nation truly grieved. I don't mean to minimize the tragedy of 9/11; the terrorist attacks have reshaped our lives in America. But I believe in the years ahead the sudden loss of economic prosperity and security will have had a much deeper impact than the threat of terrorism. Either way, the death of well-being takes time to grieve; and grieve we must.

CHAPTER
11

November 18, 2009

DJIA: 10,437.42

S&P: 1,110.32

It's a Moon Shot

I had the opportunity to witness my first space shuttle launch this week, and it truly is remarkable. The power of the rocket engines and the technology behind it all certainly speaks to the ingenuity of the innovative American mind. An event like this expands the imagination and helps you understand that perhaps America's best days are yet ahead. But the confidence to believe America can right the ship is still a very thin veneer. History has shown that it will take time to rebuild confidence in the economy, the markets and in fact, ourselves. Sometimes it just takes proof to build that confidence. So, consider this: Corporate profits are rising at the highest rate since mid 1975, and the first three quarters of this year are up an astonishing 34.8%. For all of the tentative confidence, Corporate America is performing at a very productive rate, and many believe 2010 will look better than 2009.

Yes, I know we still have problems. I would say we have historic challenges in front of us, and solutions will be a real grinding process. But the stock market has a certain momentum behind it, and a year-end rally appears to be more likely. With the Christmas season approaching, the U.S. consumer will either believe 2010 will be better and spend money, or will continue to feel gloomy and spend sparingly. I think we may be surprised by the strength in retail sales come December. Investors should continue to add to equity investments on weakness in this market.

One last anecdote that has profound long-term implications is that the gridlock in Washington may be thawing. When I saw on the news that President Obama will sit down with Fox News for an interview, well, I can only conclude that anything is possible.

November 25, 2009

DJIA: 10,433.71
S&P: 1,105.65

Thanksgiving 2009

One year ago, the financial sky was falling and the year ahead looked, well, dire. The year 2009 has, in fact, been most challenging for the vast majority of the American people. The profound change our economy is going through has had and will have historic implications not only on our nation, but on us as well. Most people have had their lives altered during this period, and I doubt these times will be forgotten soon. Yet, as I talk with friends and reflect on our year, there is much we are thankful for, and it is nearly impossible to be despairing when one has gratitude.

It's Thanksgiving, and we are still standing. Maybe a little tired, torn, and tattered, but still standing. We can give thanks for that. For many, recovery in financial terms is on the way. Emotions will take longer; they always do when trauma strikes, but we will hope, again, our economy will heal and may even become stronger.

I have been reading *Abraham Lincoln: His Essential Wisdom*. I find myself doing that from time to time, especially during the rough patches of political highway our nation travels. But I was struck by his quote on making his first dollar. President Lincoln said, "I could scarcely credit that I, a poor boy, had earned a dollar in less than a day...that by honest work I had earned a dollar. The world seemed wider and fairer before me. I was a more hopeful and confident being from that time."

On this Thanksgiving, I pray that our days ahead will help us see the world wider and fairer, and that calms us to be more hopeful and confident.

December 2, 2009

DJIA: 10,471.58
S&P: 1,108.86

Until the Music Stops

Bright lights, marching bands, and kids in reindeer costumes rang in the Christmas season in downtown Holland last night. Thousands of people lined the streets to wave at Santa as he made his way down Eighth Street. With the sounds of Christmas carols in the background, it made for some normalcy in what has been a crazy year. The question now is whether Santa will visit Wall Street to give investors some holiday cheer.

Last week we saw that the world economic system is still a little fragile, as world markets sold off on news of a debt crisis in Dubai. I don't believe this was a sustainable sell-off, but rather just a momentary break in confidence. This was a financial land mine, which reminds us of the risk still present in our world today. Investors should expect the occasional land mine like Dubai as we work our way through a deleveraging of the world economy.

This market is being driven by expectations, confidence and cash, which can be a powerful cocktail in the short run. I would like to see solid economic fundamentals to support current stock prices, but it is what it is. The more we worry about what might be, we simply miss out on a cash-driven rally, which will probably push prices higher. The question in my mind is, why not 11,000 on the Dow Jones average? With short-term interest rates at historic lows, the stock market looks more compelling, especially as our expectations of an improving economy bolsters confidence. In other words, I'm bullish until we have a clear indicator that monetary policy is going to change. There is a long list of impending problems on the horizon, and I do not want to minimize the risk. But like the game of musical chairs, it's all fun and games until the music stops. The music is still playing, so enjoy it and profit from it. Just be alert and listen for the subtle change in song.

December 9, 2009

DJIA: 10,288.97
S&P: 1,091.94

Blizzard
_____

A year-end rally would sure be nice to finish off one of the more tumultuous years in history. But there just isn't much of the year left, and a rally will have to hurry. The sideways trading is looking more like the correction we were looking for back in September, and without a catalyst, it looks like many investors will just be content with running the clock out on 2009. I would expect some volatility as institutions and traders alike prepare for 2010. In fact, there could be some profit-taking early in 2010, as some money is taken off the table from the monster rally that began in March.

The next big catalyst, of course, will be corporate earnings being reported beginning in January. By then, the Christmas shopping season will be known in terms of consumer spending, and we will see any improvement in employment. My guess is that there will be some surprising good news that develops early in the new year. There are many variables in play, and that certainly gives us, as the average investor, plenty to worry about. But that's what makes for a positive surprise, so don't get overly bearish.

It's the heavy hand of government that we all need to keep an eye on. The early signs of economic recovery can be easily squashed by counter-productive public policy. Here is a quote by my good friends at the money management firm of Norris, Perné, & French that caught my eye: "Trust is an essential ingredient in the functioning of our economic system and financial markets. Skepticism is healthy. Mistrust is corrosive." We are very near a tipping point of trust and a very corrosive political landscape.

The year 2010 is going to be very interesting in many arenas. We believe the runaway fiscal policy will impose the cruelest tax of all, which is inflation. The timing is unknown, the degree is unknown, but basic economics suggests that when you create too much of something, you diminish its value, including the U.S. dollar.

Finally, for all of you reading this today, especially in those parts of the country that are warm and sunny, we are under a blizzard warning here in Holland, and you're not. But life is always about perspective, and I will enjoy our white Christmas.

On this morning, I was particularly reflective. My journal would capture a hint of hope:

We can be restored, but I must first believe it's possible. I find restoration a difficult task to believe when my heart is discouraged and weary. The spirit of depression weighs down the heart, especially the heart of a nation, and when there is a lack of encouragement, you live life in a defensive posture. Once you are discouraged, it takes time and repeated success to be restored."

The year was beginning to wind down; the markets would meander for weeks, barely drifting in any clear direction. It is difficult to describe the weariness of most investors; broken dreams, broken jobs, and broken homes – this was the social stew the prior year had prepared. But, restored? Is it even possible to restore the Norman Rockwell version of America? Did it ever exist? I hope so. Just as I hoped the holidays would bring some cheer, some joy, some hope.

The further we traveled beyond the crisis, the more perspective I began to gain. I was sensing a new beginning; perhaps the dawn was finally here. Yet, in the back of my mind, a child's rhyme continued to haunt me: "Humpty Dumpty sat on a wall, Humpty Dumpty had a great fall..." You know the rest.

We guarded our optimism in late 2009, as we wondered if all the king's men could put this economy back together again.

I quietly stood, looking out my office windows overlooking Eighth Street in downtown Holland. There was a parade, and before me was Santa Claus, riding in a convertible with blinking lights draped all around, throwing candy as the downtown Christmas promenade kicked off the shopping season. It gets dark early in December, and with the lights, the festive mood, the dancing – the clowns and even a delivery truck all decked out with blinking lights – people lined the streets with smiles. I looked down on the crowds, wondering. Maybe Humpty had a chance after all. Sometimes, it just takes a parade.

CHAPTER
12

December 16, 2009

DJIA: 10,452.00
S&P: 1,107.93

The Calm Before...

I find myself reflecting back on 2009, and feel as though the breathtaking events in the year have been replaced by an eerie calm, which makes me both content and anxious at the same time. It's as though an economic lifetime had occurred in the past 12 months. Now we look toward 2010 and start to formulate our best guess as to the major themes to look for and profit from, despite the uncertainty of so many circumstances I have mentioned before. Today, we do not expect the Federal Reserve to stray from its current policy. We reasonably know that the current Fed policy can't last, and that the easy money of financial crisis will be removed from the system. But 2010 is an election year, and dare I say politics may play a role in Federal policy? Having just said that, look for higher interest rates in 2010 and the growing concern of inflation, which seems so obvious to many market observers.

The big story this week was in the energy sector, as Exxon makes a bid to purchase XTO Energy for a mere $31 billion. This story builds on two of the themes I see for next year. First, with the fear of inflation and an expanding world economy, the demand for reliable energy reserves and critical supplies of commodities will only grow. Secondly,

I believe that the merger and acquisition activity we have already seen will increase as economic fundamentals continue to demand productivity increases and cost control. This has a way of diminishing the supply of stocks to purchase on the exchanges. The last I checked, we have not suspended the laws of supply and demand, and with a growing amount of cash and declining amounts of issued stock to purchase, the market has built a dynamic for sustaining stock prices.

The frantic pace of events that overwhelmed many investors in 2009 should start to look more normal in 2010. I do not want to minimize the many structural problems in our government and economy, but regardless of our problems, the pace will seem manageable. I believe patience and flexibility for investors will be rewarded, as well-managed companies emerge to lead a more pronounced recovery and job growth in the second half of the year. With these themes, the average investor should consider broader diversification than in past bull markets. From emerging markets to foreign debt, and precious metals to variable-rate securities, the average portfolio will look much different. It's easier to be patient when you are broadly diversified.

December 23, 2009

DJIA: 10,464.93
S&P: 1,108.02

Hope, Dreams and Innovation

I don't know about you, but I'm tired of hearing the phrase "new normal" (more about that in a minute). Last Christmas the world looked much different. We were in a recession and we would subsequently see the U.S. economy shrink by 14%. At that time, I said that, investors "should expect news to continue to be negative. You should expect negative GDP for the fourth quarter and you should expect unemployment to increase an additional 2%-3%." All of this, of course, happened, and yet the near-collapse of the banking system brought us to the lows in March and the likely market bottom. Although I did not see the depth of the banking crisis, I did say, "We should also expect corporate earnings to remain weak in the first couple of quarters of 2009." So what about now?

Christmas 2009 has a different tone. Call it the "new normal" (I just had to say it) or call it "relief," the bottom line is that the U.S. economy is healing and growing again. The brute force of government has injected hundreds of billions of dollars into the economy with billions to come. This leaves us uncertain as to the unintended consequences of such use of federal force. Yet, Christmas 2009 has given us the gift of time; time to heal and time to gain our bearings. I look for better economic results moving into 2010, and see unemployment remaining stubbornly high, but improving. The stock market, with mountains of cash on the sidelines, should continue to find higher levels. It doesn't seem as dark this Christmas.

Even though it's December, springtime for the American spirit has begun. I see hope leading to dreams, resulting in innovative solutions to many complex issues. That, after all, is what makes us uniquely American. The American spirit is hard-wired in the entrepreneurial genetic code of free people. As a nation, we never give up, and we always look forward. Enjoy Christmas, reflect on family and friends, and don't be afraid to hope and dream.

December 30, 2009

DJIA: 10,545.41
S&P: 1,126.20

Live in a Forward Direction

For investors, 2009 has been a year of reflecting on life and what is truly important. In years to come it will be fascinating to listen to the stories of everyday America as told by our families and friends. It is through stories that future generations, our children and grandchildren, will hopefully learn from this period and gain wisdom from our folly.

Closing out this year is like turning the last page of a chapter in a great book. The anticipation builds as the story unfolds. I say great story because I believe America is great and our best days are ahead. So, as we begin 2010, we begin with a degree of confidence and a hope for better days. John Ortberg, a favorite author of mine, has said, "Life is meant to be lived in a forward direction." For the past few years, America has been playing defense, but I sense 2010 will be a year where well-managed companies will send the offensive team back on the field and play to win. That could lead to a better than expected year for the markets.

As a nation, we are not without our problems. The litany of issues is long and troubling. The largesse of government makes some investors nervous, while others seem quite comfortable with the scope of government. Despite these known concerns, it is the Federal Reserve that will be the big story of 2010. Short-term interest rates are artificially low and will have to be raised. As so often happens, the Fed has fallen behind the curve and will become reactive. In an election year, they could be slow to take tightening action. This could make for a market that drifts higher, waiting for the inevitable rate hikes to come.

We are all on inflation watch, and the market leaders that have been strong in 2009 - natural resources, energy and technology - should stay strong in 2010. Those leaders, along with better than expected corporate earnings, could be the fuel necessary to move the markets higher in the first half of the year.

Visibility for the second half of the year is poor at best. I suspect as health care, cap-and-trade, and major financial reform become clearer, we will know more about future inflation and higher taxes moving forward. I don't know what this legislation will look like, but I do know deficits and taxation are two things that could derail a bull market.

But for the moment, live in a forward direction and look for more cash to leave the sidelines and enter the markets.

January 6, 2010

DJIA: 10,572.02
S&P: 1,136.52

Know When to Hold Them

We are seeing a solid start to 2010 as the markets continue their 2009 trading pattern of drifting higher. I have guarded optimism about the first quarter, as I sense that corporate earnings will look better than expected when they are reported over the next couple of weeks.

By far, the overarching theme for this year seems to be that investors are on inflation watch, as the U.S. government is expected to run a $1.8 trillion deficit this year, which would be a two-year accumulation of an eye-popping $3 trillion of new debt. Normally, that would be disastrous for the U.S. dollar and would cause significant inflation, but these are far from normal times.

Energy prices, commodity prices, unemployment woes, and housing all serve as a counterweight to a robust economic recovery and the inevitable inflation brewing in the system. All of these factors give the Federal Reserve the political cover not to raise short-term interest rates until after the November elections. This is why the Fed will end up behind the curve in controlling inflationary pressures that printed money causes.

Sometimes, you just have to play the cards you are dealt. In this case, the market is drifting higher, being led by commodities, energy and technology. So unless or until some new cards are played, don't fight the Fed. Remember, interest rates near zero tend to be positive for stocks. I suspect over the next few months we will get quite uncomfortable with the level of the stock market, and that unease will not get better as political events clarify health care and taxes. But for the moment, I look for better than expected news, which should buoy the markets.

I was wrong. The economy was showing clear signs of recovering, which lead me to believe that the normal course of interest rates would be to rise; they would not and have not. The inflationary environment that I could see developing has been late in arriving, drawing out this season of extraordinary low interest rates. So, maybe I haven't been wrong, exactly. Just early.

In my defense, a financial crisis is like mama's special recipe: you know what it is, but you don't know all the ingredients. We knew the recession was caused by a financial crisis; we still are discovering the many ingredients that helped create this mysterious brew of collapse and uncertainty.

We were in a market that simply humbled you. Most times it felt as though we were shooting at a moving target or targets that seemed so far away. The problem was trying to keep your eye on the target, as the daily news was dominated by the new health care proposals and the impact those proposals would have on our economy.

When you watch a movie, many times the soundtrack disappears into the background. You would hear it, if you were listening for the melody, but for the most part, you watch the main story unfold, unaware of the musical score. In our case, it was the drama around healthcare, leaving the soundtrack of better-than-expected economic news playing in the background. It was hard to imagine that our national attention had swayed from the trauma of the financial crisis to politics as usual, in just 10 months. With deep partisan and philosophical divides, each party drew entrenched lines, creating a vacuum of wisdom and compromise.

Despite the political theater, the new year was set to open with an upward bias for the markets. Pent-up demand from months of consumers being scared and confused was starting to show signs of an early spring, as some confidence had returned and consumer spending started to uptick.

CHAPTER
13

January 13, 2010

DJIA: 10,627.26
S&P: 1,136.22

It's a Stair Stepper!

As Alcoa reported earnings yesterday that were under expectations, the market seemed to simply run out of gas as we saw the six-day winning streak end. But was that the reason for the markets to decline? Yesterday, we also learned that the Chinese Central Bank was taking steps to slow down the growth of credit. I give the Chinese Central Bank credit for being proactive in curbing excess, and this is a good example of a central bank getting out in front of the curve on inflationary pressures. Perhaps our own Federal Reserve should take note. At the end of the day, slower growth in China will impact the U.S. economy, as this could slow exports to Asia, and certainly higher energy prices add to our trade deficit and slows growth here in the U.S.

Both of these events, although unrelated, lead me to believe that Fed policy here in the U.S. may have some room to look at 2011 for any significant tightening of the money supply. When you look closer at Alcoa's results, you read that lower than expected earnings were attributed to higher energy costs. Is this an isolated incident, or should we expect more companies to see similar results?

A slow-growth environment eases inflationary pressures. If higher energy prices and slowing growth in Asia continue, it's hard to make a case for strong growth in the U.S. However, that doesn't mean the party is over. Slow growth could lead to a stair-step market, where we continue to drift higher in a two-step-forward and one-step-back scenario. Remember that old Wall Street adage, "Don't fight the Fed." Until the Federal Reserve changes policy, I see no reason the markets can't have an upward bias.

I am not saying to throw caution to the wind. In fact, without a strong corporate earnings season, I would expect a good market correction. Time will tell, and over the next few weeks we should have our answer. But for now, buy stocks on weakness and be patient in putting money to work.

January 20, 2010

DJIA: 10,725.43
S&P: 1,150.23

Game Changer

In the real estate world, you hear the expression "location, location, location." In the stock market, there is a similar expression, "earnings, earnings, earnings." We are in the middle of corporate earnings season, and today a number of the big banks will be reporting fourth-quarter results. So far, earnings have not been spectacular. With underperformance from the big banks, it is reasonable to presume the credit system in the U.S. is still under repair. It's also reasonable to believe a sustained economic recovery will not occur until the banking system is healthy and able to lend.

But of course, the wild card of this market happened last night in Massachusetts. Scott Brown, the Republican, won a stunning victory in the special Senate race for the seat vacated when Ted Kennedy died. The political fallout is unknown, but certainly a reassessment of public policy proposals is happening in Washington as you read this. In the words of the President, "Elections have consequences," and I would say perhaps this election is the proverbial shot across the bow for an agenda that has America very anxious and angry.

Time will tell, but with an unexpected event like this, investors will have to recalibrate what a shift in public policy means. Uncertainty has never been good for stocks. Currently, the markets are due for a correction. Prices are extended, and I think a pause is probably out there over the short run. In the event of a correction, buying on weakness seems appropriate. Remember, there is still a mountain of cash on the sidelines looking for a home.

January 27, 2010

DJIA: 10,194.29
S&P: 1,092.17

Political Mischief

"Time will tell, but, with an unexpected event like this, investors will have to recalibrate what a shift in public policy means. Uncertainty has never been good for stocks. Currently, the markets are due for a correction. "

The quote above is from last week, and little did I know that a correction as large as 5% was imminent, triggered by an upset Republican victory in Massachusetts. But was this Senate election a symptom of something greater? Much has been said about last week's election and we all have reached our own conclusions, but what strikes me is the growing credibility gap between Washington lawmakers and the American people. This credibility gap is a large contributing factor in the current market decline. Investors are looking for a much higher degree of certainty out of Washington, rather than the schizophrenic public policy we have seen proposed in the last week.

In the short run, politics trumps corporate earnings, and with this heavy dose of politics in the markets, *be cautious with the amount of risk you are taking, as I expect to see increased volatility.* I can't get too bullish until Congress and the administration clarify and articulate where they want to lead the nation.

The good news is that, in general, corporate earnings for the fourth quarter are looking better and point to a better 2010. In the long run, corporate earnings usually determine stock prices. At the end of the day, the growing frustration over political mischief is simply making investors nervous in the short term, and that for now is not a good thing.

February 3, 2010

DJIA: 10,296.85
S&P: 1,103.32

Pancakes or French Toast?

This morning on the radio, I was asked as my opening question if I preferred pancakes or french toast as the best breakfast meal. Seems like a very simple question, doesn't it? After attempting to give the host a politically correct answer on my breakfast choice (if there is such a thing), he then asked my opinion on AIG bonuses and the financial market reform working its way through Congress. Like pancakes or french toast, my response was very simple again; I am not sure what appropriate compensation should be for companies like AIG. I am not sure what financial reform should look like either. What I do know is that these issues are backward-looking and their solutions have a high degree of complexity. In other words, these are head fakes on the playing field. The American people are concerned with jobs. Washington has been tone deaf to the most basic of concerns of the American people. We sometimes make things too complex and end up missing the point all together. The U.S. economy has been showing signs of improvement, but we need better news on the employment front to see a sustained market rally and a healthy economic recovery.

The other basic concern of the American people is the growing federal government deficit. This, too, is very complex, but we all know that mounting debt is unsustainable. I will talk more about this in the next few weeks, but Zichterman & Clark Capital Management believes that one of three scenarios may play out on this issue. (1.) The U.S. government will default on its bonds. (2.) The U.S. government will default on its people. (3.) The U.S. government will monetize the debt (print money). All three scenarios have implications for investors and would call for different actions. We continue to talk through these scenarios in our morning strategy meetings, and are influencing our advice toward a more tactical approach to portfolios.

So as I think about it, maybe our economic concerns are much like the question regarding pancakes or french toast. However, we look at it, as more jobs or a lower government deficit, I say, give me a healthy portion of both.

Between Christmas and New Year of 2009, I remember going to the movies. I don't know about you, but sometimes watching a story unfold on the big screen helps me view real life with a broader perspective. Ken Gire, an author I admire, once said, "Movies are the parables of our time"; I could not agree more. On that cold December evening, I sat and viewed a modern parable, *Up in the Air*, starring George Clooney. As I watched Ryan Bingham's shallow life unfold, I found the storyline leaving me quite empty, as well as reflective. I'm not a movie critic, and certainly I'm no judge of quality cinema, however, the movie was describing a slice of our country as it is now, and that made it very interesting to me.

Up in the Air is a modern parable of a disconnected world – not physically of course, as this was a story of a man trying to fly 10 million miles for frequent flyer points, but rather it was a melancholy look at how we are farther away from each other than ever. The Great Recession had disconnected millions of people from their jobs, from their homes, and from their way of life; it had left us more anxious, more irritable and more unsure about our future. Now, 2010 was beginning, yet the freshness and hope for the new year remained up in the air.

I think that is why Scott Brown's victory in the special election for the late Ted Kennedy's empty seat was so stunning; emotionally it shook the nation. The melancholy caused by a sense of disconnection was altered by average people taking an unpredictable step and changing the apparent trajectory of history. As I look back, this was a defining moment and was the beginning of the Tea Party Movement.

CHAPTER
14

February 10, 2010

DJIA: 10,085.64
S&P: 1,070.52

The Correction Continues

This past week I have been traveling, and somewhere between Chicago and Philadelphia, I caught myself thinking that the world seemed bigger. Listening to the news and all our problems makes the world seem small and unmanageable. But spending time in airports and gazing out a window at 30,000 feet, I realize that the U.S. economy is massive. Thirteen trillion dollars worth of GDP is made up of people just like me, from people going to work providing goods and services, to people retired trying to enjoy their senior season. But every transaction, large or small, contributes to the $13 trillion of economic activity. Often, we get caught up in the daily moves of Wall Street and lose sight of the overall size of our economy. Ultimately, keeping a broad perspective is an essential part of being an investor in this day and age.

As a part of that broad perspective, last week I touched on the consequence of a ballooning national debt. The current threat to markets seems to be a sovereign debt concern, specifically in the small nation of Greece. Deficits do matter and will have consequences to currency. In the U.S., I mentioned three possible outcomes, and suggested printing money is the political path of least resistance and a probable scenario in addressing our own deficit problems. Printing money, or monetizing debt as economists like to say, will have consequence. The likely outcome of this national behavior is normally some degree of inflation. We believe a broad perspective for investors should include a modest to high degree of inflation here in the U.S. History has shown that inflation has the greatest chance of disrupting the standard of living. Inflation is the cruelest tax of any nation, and needs to be respected when looking at your portfolio. My only question (call it a concern) is this: Will the economy experience a second recession before the consequence of printing money hits? Time will tell.

Although not a current problem, we have been suggesting that more investors position themselves for future inflation. For now, we are cautious as the market correction continues. But despite the current markets, we continue to like energy, natural resources and agriculture as areas to include in your portfolio and would not be afraid to selectively buy on weakness.

February 17, 2010

DJIA: 10,268.81
S&P: 1,094.87

Another One-Day Wonder?

After yesterday's 1.7% gain in the Dow Jones averages, you are left wondering if this was just a one-day wonder in the volatile three-week correction we have been experiencing. A follow-through rally today would help me believe the correction has ended with a whimper instead of a bang. Now, the question is: Will we approach the market highs we saw in January? Momentum has been negative, but as we have seen, the markets have been able to turn on a dime and reverse course in just days.

Since the Massachusetts Senate election, the markets have seen the deepest correction since the March 2009 lows. What is interesting is that the usual suspects of recent sell-offs (political uncertainty, slowing economies, mounting debt problems, and currency swings) have largely hidden the positive results of corporations for the fourth quarter. Statistics are showing that more than 70% of corporations reporting earnings have beaten expectations, and 60% have beaten revenue projections. The fundamentals are showing signs of improvement and could help the markets regain some traction.

If we are looking for more fuel to ignite a new rally, consider this report: U.S. nonfinancial corporations are sitting on the largest percentage of cash to assets in more than 50 years. Yesterday, it was reported that Simon Properties made a $10 billion bid for rival General Growth Properties. As I have said before, one event does not make a trend, but I can't help thinking that corporate cash could lead to a new wave of mergers and acquisitions, which could further advance the markets.

I still sense headwinds for a market rally. However, stock prices have pulled back to levels that look attractive again. Selective buying would seem to make sense, especially if today is a positive one.

February 24, 2010

DJIA: 10,282.41
S&P: 1,094.60

The Stock Market Charged With a DUI

Have you ever been behind a driver under the influence? Careening from one side of the road to the other, driving slow then driving fast? I think we are seeing that type of behavior from our current markets. Yesterday, consumer confidence fell well below expectation, dropping below 50%. The FDIC reported that banks posted their sharpest decline in lending since 1942. It also said that bank failures continue at record pace, with 1 out of 11 banks experiencing problems. With this news, it's not hard to see how the markets are having trouble staying on the road.

But here is the question: Are these leading indicators or lagging indicators? I think we know this recovery is going to be quite modest. Many are suggesting a jobless recovery, which only makes for a more difficult recovery. Having said that, should we be surprised that consumer confidence is falling? When you consider the political uncertainty of economic and tax policy not only from Washington, but also state and local governments, it should not be surprising that consumers are uneasy.

In Holland, Michigan, we are surrounded by well-managed companies and an entrepreneurial spirit that has overcome hard times before. Maybe that's why Holland was voted the second-happiest place to live. I say this to point out that despite the economic news, despite the volatility in the markets, and despite the uncertainty facing us, history has shown that well-managed companies will reward investors over the long run. Whether it's with rising dividends or rising stock prices, certain companies have persevered. We are in a market that is struggling to stay on the road, and responsible investors are finding this very frustrating. But this market will eventually sober up. We continue to see a range-bound market weaving up and down, and I would expect a major move up or down to be event-driven. I just don't know what that event will be; and with a long list of usual suspects, my advice is to drive defensively.

March 3, 2010

DJIA: 10,405.98
S&P: 1,118.31

From There to Here

Quietly, this market has been improving; scraping and clawing its way back to even for the year. Sometimes our current struggles are best defined by our past, and although investors are frustrated by the lack of progress in 2010, what a difference a year makes. As we begin the month of March, I can't help but reflect back on where we were just 12 months ago. Here is an excerpt from my March 4, 2009, message to investors:

Are We There Yet?

Looking at indicators, which are showing the markets are oversold at levels similar to October's and November's, it seems as if this week could establish a near-term low. In a time where the average investor becomes anxious, discouraged and panicked, remember to be prepared for oversold opportunities...

The Dow Jones average was at 6,726 on that day, and as we now know, the market has risen just more than 54%, or up 3,679 points to 10,405. The days in March 2009 were dark for investors here in the U.S. and around the world. Fear and uncertainty were emotional commodities shared by all. Yet, investors who persevered have seen astounding gains from the rubble of their statements in the past 12 months. The headline "Are We There Yet?" has lost the desperation we all were feeling at that time.

So, for investors looking at the rest of the year, remember that the tailwinds of a dramatically oversold market are behind us, and the headwinds of the Great Recession hangover will create a wandering market - without GPS. Certainly there are positives, as corporations are buying back stock and raising dividends, but we urge investors to not get complacent and remain opportunistic. This year will hand us new problems and with them will come new opportunities.

March 10, 2010

DJIA: 10,564.83
S&P: 1,140.45

Back to the Future

There is this nagging thought that continues to play in my mind like a never ending feedback loop. It's similar to watching a movie and thinking, "I have read the book this movie was based on." Although the movie is not exactly like the book, it is certainly familiar, much like our current economic situation. Consider this quote from a book I'm reading, *Confessions of a Price Controller:*

"Inflation is the number-one problem for the American people and for the world. It disrupts economic, social and political systems. And if not checked, it increases the cry for a shift from a market-driven economy to one that is more centrally directed - to one where price and wage controls are not intermittent or in phases, but continuous as a part of an overall planned, mixed economy."

Many of you reading this have expressed the concerns found in the previous quote. The subtle anxiety of deficits and the consequences created from them have given us all sleepless nights, if not certainly restless nights. But this quote is saying more than you think. Although it reads like the current headlines, it was written in April of 1974. The author, Jack Grayson, was chairman of the Price Commission for President Richard Nixon. In other words, the current narrative is from an old movie that's playing again.

Every portfolio, whether it be conservative or aggressive, needs to remain mindful of what inflation can do to your standard of living. We are working hard crafting solutions to assist our clients in finding the right balance to meet their income needs and growth objectives. We have a number of ideas to diversify a portfolio in current times. We may be early in our concern for wage and price controls, but when the signs are present, an early warning system demands action. Many of you have made incremental changes in your accounts as appropriate. Like you, I wonder: Where's my 1974 almanac?

I think at one time or another we all have had our exposure to Greek mythology. These parables capture the nuances of the ancient world, but they also demonstrate the strength and sophistication of early Greek culture and the role it plays in Western culture today.

In early 2010, the wrath of the Greek gods would strike with the power of Zeus: Greece was, in modern terms, bankrupt as a result of overindulgent public policies. It was the kind of profligacy that would anger the gods of the European Central Banks and the European parliaments.

Greek unions staged a second strike, aimed directly at their parliament, over massive budget cuts. The ballooning debt had overwhelmed the government's ability to manage, yet after years of living well beyond their means, the Greek people were face to face with a depression-era reality—austerity. Riots broke out. Banks were firebombed. People died. The Greeks seemed willing to destroy their country rather than embrace frugality.

I couldn't help but wonder, was there a Greek lesson in this for America? Will we see similar types of union activism and demonstrations as our own form of American austerity begins? We were already beginning to hear about large state deficits, especially in California. For Greece and California, the similarities appear to be eerily close. Greece, by all reasonable measures has hit the tipping point; for California, time will tell.

For the United States, the transfer of private debt to public debt has been stunning. The acceleration and accumulation of debt will have long-term consequences, as the choices available for our government to manage this debt continues to dwindle. We don't know what the tipping point will be because we don't know when the expansion of government debt is unsustainable. I suspect debasing our currency by printing more of it to meet our obligations is the path of least political resistance.

I would also say it's the most dangerous.

CHAPTER
15

March 17, 2010

DJIA: 10,685.98
S&P: 1,159.46

What's on Your List?

I'm a reluctant optimist. Or, said another way, I'm an optimist who worries. Bull markets always climb a wall of worry, and this market has been no exception. Recently, clients from out of state traveled to Holland to discuss *The List:* their list of significant risks. Their question, of course, was "How will this list affect our portfolio?" We all have our list, and as investors, we must recognize that there will always be one. I suspect you haven't necessarily written it down, but it's there, your own personal list of "what ifs." Sometimes your list whispers, and sometimes, like now, it screams at you. Risk and uncertainty seem to always be involved with opportunities. Yes, we all have our lists, whether the market goes up or down.

It is interesting to me, however, that the list is not what I worry about. I worry most about the unknown; those things that haven't even made the list. Usually, the random events or the social reaction to economic dealings are what most unnerve us and cause the greatest gains or losses. Do I worry about inflation, higher taxes and the national debt? Yes. I even worry about the Chicago Cubs winning the World Series. How crazy is that? Here is my point: you need a list. What risk to your portfolio keeps you up at night? What risk could most affect your standard of living in retirement?

I believe inflation could be the greatest risk confronting investors moving into 2011. It is unknown what the consequences from the unprecedented government intervention of the last 18 months will be. So, you plan for what you know and stay diversified for the unknown events. There is a growing complacency creeping into this market, and, like the eye of the storm, you should prepare for the risk you worry about most. The world seems more volatile, and the negative surprise can happen at any time. We continue to believe flexibility for managers of mutual funds is preferable, especially in these times.

(1) Reduction / Elimination of Social Security

2 2011 TAX INCREASE (Bush tax cuts gone)

3 Federal Debt / Dollar Decline / Inflation

(4) Health Insurance costs

5 Length of Recession (Double Dip?)

6 Iran War / Terrorist Attack

March 24, 2010

DJIA: 10,888.83

S&P: 1,174.17

What Else Can I Say?

I suspect when it comes to health care, I can't possibly give a fresh analysis to what has possibly become the longest running episode of the reality TV show *Survivor*. Truly, the drama Congress served up over the weekend was the quality of a made-for-TV movie, and the sad fact is, it may not be over. It will take time to discern the direct and unintended consequences of this 2,300-page piece of legislation. But what we do know is that a significant change in public policy affecting 16% of the U.S. economy will create new winners and losers. Time will tell as to whether we have broken new ground in health care coverage or if we really have tinkered at the margins. However, the realities of higher taxes and larger government deficits are sure to ripple through the economy; they always do.

Here is the good news: The U.S. economy is bigger than Washington. The American spirit is alive, clearly frustrated, but still dreaming and innovating, and I believe it will overcome the obstacles Washington creates. I am concerned about the government sprawl into the private sector, but this is not new. History has shown us other times when government rapidly grew, and millions of creative

Americans found ways to create economic growth. It can happen again.

In the short run, we must remember that the Federal Reserve is being very accommodative with artificially low interest rates, and with the Federal stimulus plan having hundreds of billions of dollars yet to spend, it will not be hard for the economy to experience a sugar high over the next couple quarters. But easy money by the Fed will have consequences; again, history shows us that. Inflation, although not currently a problem, is a consequence of easy money. Inflation undermines the value of assets and money and diminishes the value of our currency abroad. I hope I am wrong, and that higher taxes, larger government, and easy money by the Fed will create a stronger economy and lower unemployment, but I can't rewrite history. Hope and change is a narrative we want to believe. It was true in the 1930s, the 1960s and 1970s. Good intentions are honorable, but the natural laws of economics can't be denied.

March 31, 2010

DJIA: 10,907.42
S&P: 1,173.27

One Shining Moment

March is exciting! For basketball fans, it's a time of full immersion into college basketball, and words like "bracketology" actually makes sense. The games are unpredictable, yet hope is alive regardless of your seeding. Each game has its moments of momentum. Momentum is the proverbial wild card of any game, creating giants out of the small and making the invincible helpless. March has been exciting, and like the NCAA tournament, the stock market has had a run of momentum.

Momentum rarely lasts for an entire game, and when looking at our current stock market, you can feel the momentum starting to wane. With the Dow Jones average up more than 6% for the month of March, it is only reasonable to think a breather is close at hand. But there are reasons to look favorably on the next few quarters. Why do I say that? Let's look at copper prices, the yield on a 30-year Treasury bond, and gasoline prices.

First, copper prices are at their highest since June of 2008. Copper is a good barometer of manufacturing strength for an economy. Second, the 30-year Treasury yield is at 4.75%, the highest rate since October of 2007. Finally, gasoline prices are once again pushing $3 per gallon. All three data points are interesting, as they suggest optimism in corporate America and the consumer.

There are reasons to believe the markets could work their way higher. (Higher as in pre-panic levels.) An additional 5% to 10% this year is possible, given the economic dynamics already in the pipeline. Therefore, to patiently buy on weakness makes for a reasonable strategy over the next month or so.

The theme song for the NCAA basketball tournament is "One Shining Moment," and it is traditionally played at the conclusion of the final game when a new champion is crowned. It's a moving rendition for the hard work, great plays, and perseverance of the tournament. Well, for investors, the Panic of 2008 is behind us, and it's time to cue the music.

My day began with a morning phone call from clients who were also friends of mine. The news had been particularly shrill with deepening partisan sides drawing disparate conclusions for a vision of America to come. My friend asked if I had time to see them later that day. They live in Northern Indiana, and I am in Holland, Michigan; this would be a 2½-hour drive for them to meet with me. I suspected their anxious thoughts on numerous issues were deeply troubling them and that they would need my counsel. What apprehension would be so urgent to make someone drive five hours for a meeting with their financial advisor on this day in March 2010, on such short notice?

That afternoon we met and reviewed their list of specific concerns and the effect on their retirement plans. I should add that my clients had retired in 2008; the financial trauma that had followed was an emotional earthquake, as their life savings and retirement security was obliterated in a matter of months. The good news was they were prepared for some level of calamity, so they had a little time to ride out the storm. But they sensed a new storm coming, and for that, they weren't sure they were quite as ready.

I'm always amazed at Middle America; there is something wholesome about that way of life. Small towns, big hearts, and a love of their country come to mind. Their list, which we reviewed, was the result of a culmination of daily 30-second shallow thoughts of a modern media being forced into the lives of good, decent people who believed in a decent and good America. The media messages so often have the intent to incite, rather than inform; on this occasion, I think the list was representative of how millions of Americans were viewing the world.

Different points of view are nothing new in this country. Political philosophy has been quite diverse over the years, but I sensed something different with my meeting in March to discuss their list.

The specific questions on the concerns presented were spot on, getting to the point in a straightforward way. What did not appear on the list, but was the subtle message I would reflect on days later, was the growing divide, which I believe is the quiet epidemic of a cultural virus that we have seen in America on rare occasions.

This divide of what America should be is growing wide and deep in 2011 and history would suggest it will not end well. The great tensions of our republic have always been from dissension from within rather than from a foreign enemy.

The question I had then and remains today is: How will we close the divide? I believe in American greatness and the ability of free people rallying to overcome great obstacles, yet I don't believe it will be our greatness that closes this divide. I believe only our goodness can heal our nation.

What's on your list?

CHAPTER
16

April 7, 2010

DJIA: 10,969.99

S&P: 1,189.44

Do You Sense Some Urgency?

I saw a headline this morning that seems to be a contradiction to the prevailing deflationary theme of many economists. The headline read "Time to Buy a House?". The story is significant not because of the headline, but rather because of the perception noted in the polls of consumers. One poll said that two-thirds of Americans believe prices for housing will be the same or higher in the next 12 months. Perception can be powerful in the behavior of consumers - they don't have to be accurate.

The seeds of inflation are being sown... I don't know the timing, but I am certain that the natural laws of economics will unfold. In the political arena, you can spin the facts and suspend logic, but, ultimately, we know that when you manufacture more money, you will inflate it. What has been missing from the inflation story is evidence of the acceptance that a growing money supply will have consequences of higher prices. Consumers expecting housing prices to rise in the next 12 months may be the first sign that there is a change of perception. History shows us that when we believe prices will be higher, there is certain urgency in spending. This urgency can create a spiral of increasing prices.

Remember, perceptions can be powerful - they don't have to be accurate.

Speaking of higher prices, the markets continue to be favorable for taking risk. In the short run it would seem natural to see a correction; the markets have had a very strong run in the last six weeks. Will we see 11,000 on the Dow Jones averages? I believe we will. However, with corporate earnings season beginning next week, fundamentals, rather than momentum, could be the catalyst for the next leg up or the beginning of a correction.

April 14, 2010

DJIA: 11,019.42
S&P: 1,197.30

Play Ball

Spring training has ended and the season begins. For baseball fans, each season begins with renewed optimism, which in my case, being a Cubs fan, is not always well-founded. But be that as it may, first-quarter corporate earnings season also began this week, and already we have seen Intel and JP Morgan hit the ball out of the park, as they reported better than expected results. I am looking for the next few weeks to be filled with a powerful display of earnings and the home crowd cheering as the markets drift toward their pre-panic levels of 2008.

There are two events that loom on the horizon of which I feel we must remain mindful. First, the November midterm elections could have a profound impact on the economy and markets. It is too early to predict a change of agenda or direction, but clearly there is unrest in the electorate. Second, and maybe more obvious, will be the inevitable change of Fed policy that has contributed to the rebound in the markets. The "easy money" policy of the Federal Reserve has created an environment for stocks that is favorable for higher prices. We don't know when the policy will change, but higher interest rates could become competition for stocks, and that could end, or at least limit, the party.

Until we see a change in the broader themes of better corporate earnings and interest rates remaining at historic lows, I have to favor stocks.

April 21, 2010

DJIA: 11,117.06

S&P: 1,207.17

Foul Ball

I was driving home the other day and passed by the elementary school, where a few dads were coaching their very young children in how to play baseball. I thought about the basics, simple fundamentals of playing the game. Investing can be like that. You keep your strategy simple, focus on the fundamentals, and allocate according to your investment objectives.

Unlike the simplicity of Little League baseball, where kids learn to keep their gloves down and develop a level swing, we learned last week that the game of investing may not be so easy. The financial engineering and sophistication of Wall Street has made investing anything but simple. After all, what is a CDO or a derivative contract any way? But as complex as the financial system is, it is still quite simple from this point of view: Do you trust the markets?

Do you trust that the game is fair or not? The SEC decision last week forces market participants to ask that question. Time will tell... it always does. In the short run, financial reform is taking the oxygen out of the room, and that is making the markets look a little tired. Despite the negative headlines, we remain tentative buyers on weakness. For the long run, which really means November, we continue on inflation watch and believe higher interest rates await us in 2011.

Five thousand feet below the warm waters of the Gulf of Mexico there was a problem with the blow-out preventer connected to the Deepwater Horizon drilling rig. The operation was reportedly permitted to drill to 18,000 feet, but BP may have been drilling as deep as 25,000 feet. The early warning signs were probably abundant, yet drilling continued until the morning of April 20, 2010.

A tragic accident roughly 41 miles off the shores of Louisiana would begin a chain of events that to date has not ended. The environmental disaster had a subtle beginning; its long-term consequences remain speculation.

All told, 11 workers would lose their lives; in addition, 16 workers were injured. The rig would burn and subsequently sink, with 99 workers rescued unharmed.

The analysis started immediately. Obviously, there had been a problem: oil could be seen immediately floating on the water; however, the loss of life was the original story. The financial markets had little reaction to the disaster and were trading more on news out of Europe than on the oil spill.

In fact, this was a non-story for the markets, at least for the first 30 days. It would take that long watching the plume of oil gush from the floor of the Gulf of Mexico to realize how large this disaster would be. The economic impact was massive; the bureaucratic response by government agencies was slow and symbolic of the economic recovery.

When I think about the ballooning debt crisis, I reflect back to the Deepwater Horizon. When I picture the oil gushing from the floor of the gulf, I also think about the billions of U.S. dollars being spent and created. In both cases, we didn't have the capacity to stop the flow.

Sometimes, we learn lessons from the most disparate situations. Here is a case where an oil spill disaster has had an environmental effect on the scale of the 1930s Dust Bowl, while the creation of money and accumulation of government debt is rivaling the dire consequences of the Great Depression.

We don't know to this day what environmental impact the millions of barrels of oil will have as it lurks on the floor of the gulf, and likewise it will be years before we know the monetary impact the debt crisis will have.

We only know we didn't stop it in time.

CHAPTER
17

April 28, 2010   DJIA: 10,991.99
                                  S&P: 1,183.71

Big-Time Wrestling

We never know for sure what triggers a sell-off like yesterday's. Was it the ongoing debt problems of Greece? The smack-down grudge match in the U.S. Senate? Or was the market simply ready for some profit-taking? We have an interconnected financial world, which has issues that can be explained in hindsight, but difficult to see at that particular moment. What is clear at this time is that corporate America is having a banner earnings season, which was discounted yesterday for the usual suspects of worry. In fact, it seems that the basic diet of a bull market is a steady course of worry.

So what about yesterday's grudge match in the Senate? Well, I simply don't believe that big-time wrestling is real, and similarly, the Senate hearings on financial reform seemed staged as well. Is it troubling that the very senators who wish to reregulate our markets have an obvious shallow understanding of how the financial markets work? It sure is. Is it troubling that the investment banking industry seems shadowy and rife with conflicts of interest? Absolutely. But I would compare it to this: I love sausage for breakfast, but I don't want to see it made. The same can be said for the creation of financial instruments. The hearings yesterday at best were political theater, and at worst, show that Wall Street and Washington are out of tune with the American people. At the end of the day, we don't need villains, we need heroes. The truth is that you will need to look to Main Street for those heroes, not Washington or Wall Street.

Today, the big news will be no real news coming out of the FOMC meeting. Interest rates should remain low for the foreseeable future. Low interest rates and strong corporate earnings make the environment favorable for continued stock price gains. Although sell-offs can be normal, the trend is still our friend. Look for pullbacks to be buying opportunities.

May 5, 2010

DJIA: 10,968.97

S&P: 1,173.60

Three Strikes Eurout

The term "tipping point" has been used to describe an irreversible point in time when an incremental increase displaces equilibrium or stability. It's hard not to see a tipping point in Europe, as the nation of Greece has reached the point of too much debt, too much government spending, and too many entitlement programs to sustain itself. We are seeing frightful signs that the collective governments of Europe cannot contain the fiscal crisis that threatens the euro. The interconnectedness of the world's economies is sometimes hard to comprehend and certainly difficult to predict. But what financial markets are implying is that a financial pandemic could be spreading out of the Mediterranean.

Markets here in the U.S. have been signaling a correction for weeks. The preponderance of good earnings reports coming from Wall Street seems overwhelmed by the wave of exogenous events in Europe and the very real threat of home-grown terrorism. Investors need to be opportunistic in the face of crisis, but *patience may be the key ingredient.*

It may not be said, but many can sense that the economic recovery currently under way here in the U.S. is still somewhat fragile. However, with the crisis in Europe, the U.S. dollar has been a safe haven and may be creating an opportunity to buy natural resource-related investments that have corrected significantly in the past week on the strengthening dollar. I remain concerned with the real possibility of inflation. Inflation may be the only tool central governments have the will to use to combat the rising tide of debt most countries are accumulating. Be cautious in the short run as the correction may take a few weeks to play out.

May 12, 2010

DJIA: 10,748.26
S&P: 1,155.79

The Twins of Reality

I find it ironic that as Europe fights to keep the European Union from imploding, the safe haven is the U.S. dollar. Who would have thought you could print trillions of new dollars and have their value, in relative terms, increase? What is very telling is that the price of gold continues to hit all-time highs, as world currencies are in this state of flux. With the world printing money like a great big game of Monopoly, it is hard to not see gold remaining as an alternative for government reserve funds and a safe harbor for many investors.

The fallout of last Thursday's market collapse and recovery highlights that risk and volatility are ever present in the financial world. The tide is simply not going to gently raise all boats as we saw in the 1990s. In fact, it was a tech-nological tsunami that overwhelmed our markets and provided a spectacular sell-off not seen since 1987. We are seeing the brutal complexity of the modern financial world... A world where governments and regulatory agencies are simply overmatched by technology and too slow to react to second-by-second movement of capital. Investors continue to feel uneasy about the system, and rightfully so, but I would not overlook the better than expected earnings we are seeing in many U.S. companies.

As for the U.S. stock market, I continue to believe the cor-rection that began two weeks ago will continue for a while. Patience should be rewarded, as the volatility we are seeing in stock prices could give you an opportunity to buy the dips. Until we see a change in Federal Reserve policy, I have to favor stocks over cash.

May 19, 2010   DJIA: 10,510.95
                                 S&P: 1,120.80

Waiting for That Shoe to Drop

I don't know about you, but there are times when I
just get weary of having to worry about the world.
Market corrections, which tend to occur suddenly,
cause the markets and investors to focus on the
negatives and allow fear to trump greed in the
moment. As always, keeping perspective is critical
in assessing a buying or selling decision.

This current correction is about three weeks old and
has not only affected stocks, but also currencies
and commodities. For example, a barrel of oil has
declined more than 16%, while copper has declined
more than 20%. Investors have taken profits and
seem to be poised for the worst to happen... It
seems that there is a sense of waiting for the next
shoe to drop.

What are we missing? Well, corporate profits for
the first quarter have been very good, and many
companies are issuing favorable outlooks. Corporate
profit margins are expanding for the first time in
two years, and interest rates should remain low for
the balance of this year. Speaking of energy, lower
prices at the pump act like a tax cut for consumers
just as we enter the summer travel season. These

are not characteristics of bear markets, but they do tend to show us the way forward after a correction.

I don't mean to minimize the macro problems facing world economies, as they are formidable. However, it is probably a mistake to get overly bearish if you are a long-term investor. Market corrections are a time to prepare to put money to work. Unless the favorable trends dissipate, I have to be cautiously optimistic about a summer rally.

May 26, 2010

DJIA: 10,043.75
S&P: 1,074.03

Was That a Shark?

It appears as though a tremendous amount of fear has been discounted in today's market. In the month of May we have witnessed volatility not seen since the March lows of 2009. In fact, at 9:45 a.m. yesterday the Dow Jones average had lost 1,500 points in roughly 30 days. That stunning decline has created a market that looks to be deeply oversold and a short-term bounce would seem in order. However, geopolitical events in Europe and Korea make for a dicey landscape that has a rare mix of numerous opportunities and financial land mines. Like walking on a sheet of ice, investors are having to move cautiously through these times.

When investors are faced with uncertainty, the first instinct is to move to safety. Likewise when you are drowning you reach for the life preserver. However, sometimes we mistake the shark for a life preserver, and I'm afraid the flight to government bonds could be just that. It is hard to not see a new bubble being created in the bond market. In the near term it may seem to be the right move, but I'm afraid it's the shark. Remember, when interest rates go up, bond values decline, and what appeared safe will look quite risky.

We continue to believe, given what we currently know, that this decline in stocks has been a needed correction for a market that had been in a steep recovery from the March 2009 lows. A bull market will climb a wall of worry for an extended period of time. Bull markets end when the vast majority of investors believe their money should be in stocks not bonds. It seems to me that it makes more sense to buy good quality companies with strong balance sheets and track records of growth, rather than buying bonds of a deeply indebted nation. The question for now remains: Is it safe to go back into the water?

It was during the children's parade on May 6, with all of the children of Holland dressed in their Dutch costumes marching alongside their classmates with a full complement of local school marching bands, that the market anomaly occurred. I remember being at my desk watching CNBC while listening to the bands and kids go by; but something wasn't right. The Dow Jones average began to plunge. In the course of five minutes, a severe financial air pocket collapsed the market; 300, 500, and finally 900 points down, the collapse evaporated billions of dollars worth of equity in the time it took the children of Jefferson Elementary School and the eighth-grade band to pass by my window.

The sudden collapse would be followed by a spectacular rebound; 100, 300, and finally recovering 600 points, while outside the Tulip Time children's parade blissfully went by.

This five-minute event would be labeled the "Flash Crash." Considering the nearly 1,000-point swing, investors once again were dealing with an uncertainty difficult to quantify.

The old Wall Street adage of "sell in May – and go away" was once again beating in my head as the Holland High band performed its classic march "Tip-Toe Through The Tulips" outside my window.

Investors will tolerate many things; they understand a Ponzi scheme as an act of greed and arrogance or a miss in corporate earnings causing the value of shares to be discounted. But the Flash Crash represented something all together different. The Flash Crash was a breach of basic fairness and trust, essential qualities for a financial system and for markets that are supposed to allow investors an efficient way to trade their ownership. The real question is, if the markets are rigged, then what? High-frequency trading would be the suspect; trading in milliseconds was not an option for normal investors, but it was something shadowy institutions were able to exploit.

The damage was done, however, as the wall of worry grew taller and the uncertainty over a fair market created more anxiety in a trauma-filled environment.

CHAPTER
18

June 2, 2010

DJIA: 10,024.02
S&P: 1,070.71

The Widening Gap

"Sell in May and go away" is an old Wall Street saying that speaks to the seasonality of investing. This May certainly would have been a good time to go away, as we saw the worst performance for stocks since February of 2009. Now the debate appears to fluctuate between "are we in a new bear market?" or "is this just a correction?" At this point, the evidence would suggest we have a correction in process. How long the correction will take is simply a guess, but it is common in a correction for stocks to disconnect from economic realities, creating a gap between perception and fundamentals. A widening gap between fundamentals and perception tends to be a reflection of uncertainty in the markets, and we know the litany of uncertainties is long and varied. This widening gap becomes fertile soil for a summer rally as the markets continue to be in oversold territory.

We know the list of trouble spots: Europe has a debt crisis; BP can't stop the oil pumping into the gulf; China is slowing; and taxes are sure to rise here in the U.S. (and that's just for starters). But, a look at the news this morning suggests to me this gap exists. Consider the following taken from the news: U.S. manufacturing grew at a brisk pace last month; Germany's economy appears to be gaining steam; construction spending rose 27% in April; 77% of the S&P 500 companies beat their first-quarter earnings estimates; and, finally, gas-price declines have given consumers more income to spend. When you get this kind of disparate information, you tend to be cautious and uncertain, which in my experience is what makes a correction scary - the good news gets lost in the bad.

This is not a time to throw caution to the wind and start buying stocks with reckless abandon, but I am saying this market looks oddly better than it feels. As time passes here in June and the gap between fundamentals and perceptions widens, you should look to be a selective buyer. However, here is my disclaimer: I think the economic recovery I just described is very fragile. The risk of "what we don't know" is real and needs to be given respect. A good correction has all the ingredients for recovery, but also to deliver pain. Understand your own risk tolerance and look for opportunities to develop. We continue to like the energy and commodity areas, as many companies highly rated by Raymond James have been adversely affected by events in the Gulf of Mexico.

June 9, 2010

DJIA: 9,939.98
S&P: 1,062.00

"I Feel the Earth Moving Under My Feet..." (Carole King)

Is all of the bad news priced into this market? As we continue to bounce along six-month lows in the market you can't help but consider whether we are entering a new phase in the bull market that began in March of last year, or is this simply a correction and over the next several weeks the markets will find some stability and begin a summer rally? Either way, the confusion caused by the heavy burden of uncertainty continues to create a market that is more controlled by computers and less by individual investors. One point I will make is that history has shown time and time again that you never want to sell short the American people. Although many people are tentative and cautious about the economy, I believe the dream of many entrepreneurs is quietly alive and well, simply waiting for their moment of opportunity to present itself.

Each week that passes without a clear direction for the market creates an atmosphere in which the markets just muddle along waiting for the next big event. That could be corporate earnings being released starting in July or some other event not on the radar. Most likely it is that investors are waiting for the November midterm elections to give a clue as to what 2011 and beyond will look like. Unfortunately, we probably will have politics re-enter the investment landscape this summer with a vengeance, adding to an already volatile situation.

Jeff Saut is the Chief Market Strategist at Raymond James & Associates and I find Jeff's comments constructive this week. He commented that the markets continue to trade in and around key strategic and technical levels, which makes him cautious. For the short run, he recommends that investors should stay on defense. I would agree with that assessment, as the floor of this correction does not feel like bedrock. Any move in this market that takes us below the February lows would suggest a series of lower lows and lower highs. Hopefully, we avoid that scenario, and the evidence and voice of a sustained recovery will be seen and heard. I'm hoping for a summer rally, but I am looking over my shoulder.

June 16, 2010   DJIA: 10,404.77
                                 S&P: 1,115.23

Was That a Fog Horn?

This morning, a heavy fog has rolled in off Lake Michigan, making visibility very difficult. It is the perfect backdrop for the markets today. We are beginning another corporate earnings season, and as we look toward second-quarter results I think it is fair to say "visibility" will be a good descriptor of what we will learn. With the numerous unknowns piling up, we seem to have a financial fog that creates a tentative market and a perfect balance of bulls and bears. It may be November before the fog begins to lift.

As for yesterday's 200-point advance for the Dow Jones average, I think it falls into the category of "relief rally," as many stocks over the past five weeks had reached very oversold levels. A sustainable summer rally is possible; however it will take some positive surprises that currently have been quite elusive. Perhaps corporate earnings or better employment data will be the catalyst for a rally, but then again, it's hard to see in this fog.

What am I focused on? There are three main issues:

1. Earnings. Have the recent Eurozone problems and the rising dollar created a shift in corporate profitability?

2. Affordable energy. The Gulf Coast oil crisis has become a defining event for the administration. The effectiveness of the administration and the confidence investors take from policy decisions may create an environment that could affect consumer confidence. Knee-jerk policy decisions tend to have unintended consequences. Despite the rhetoric, you can not suspend the laws of economics and the power of supply and demand. If you cut energy supply and demand does not fall, then prices will rise. (That would be bad for consumers and a recovery.)

3. Financial regulation. It is expected that Congress will have put the finishing touches on a financial regulation package. Too heavy a hand by legislators or too light a hand could make us all cynical - or should I say, more cynical - about the whole process.

For investors who are long-term oriented, stay patient and cautious and look for investable themes to unfold. Currently, energy and inflation are two themes that I believe continue to develop.

June 23, 2010

DJIA: 10,293.52
S&P: 1,095.32

A Reflective Investor

In March of 2008 the federal government coordinated the clean-up of the investment bank Bear Stearns. We now know that Bear Stearns would be the first financial domino to fall, creating a cascade highly leveraged and very misunderstood by government and consumers alike. As I watch the daily futility of good intentions in the Gulf of Mexico, I realize that the scars of crisis takes time to put into proper context and to fully appreciate the significant changes that are brought about. When you see crisis after crisis, you begin to question more and more. You question leadership, you question the role of government, and, more important, you question what is the role and place for America in a world that seemingly becomes more dangerous and less predictable.

For investors, the long and arduous journey from the market highs of 2007 has left most wearied, and on any given day, wanting to withdraw and quit the game. Clearly, what had been normal is not, what was safe may not be, and daily volatility may be our only certainty. Yet, as Americans, we are not strangers to times such as these. We have overcome before, and I suspect we will overcome again. History would suggest that, and this may be one of those rare times when looking back is our way forward.

We fail to recognize or appreciate that history is created daily. Each day, assessments are made and trends are discovered or confirmed, leading us to a personal conclusion. For many, the basic belief is grounded in the assumption that there is a current of hope that is an abundant resource of a free nation and that sustains our democracy. But, unlike the Deep Horizon well in the gulf, the flow of optimism has lost some pressure, as we find ourselves in a time when hope and history fail to rhyme, creating a chasm of opposing realities.

Today, I believe, politics is trumping economics, and the difficult choices that need to be made to grow our economy are being lost in a dysfunctional Washington. Economic policy, good and bad, will generally bring about a fair market, much like a broken clock is right twice a day. But, in my mind, the current policies, if allowed to go unimpeded, could have far-reaching dislocations of capital and a profound impact on our current way of life. Unless our policymakers alter the current trajectory, it is more likely we will repeat the mistakes of the late '70s. Many of us remember the national malaise at that time. We were a nation held hostage on many fronts, political and economic. The narrative that would make you believe that all of our problems are unprecedented and somehow unfixable is wrong and diminishes the greatness of our nation and the heroic efforts of past leaders.

The fireworks weren't what they had been, even a year ago. Last July, a dazzling display of streaking rockets and exploding clouds falling brilliantly in celebration had delighted the whole town. And a year ago, we were climbing out of a deep hole of despair, clinging on the gains made from the lows, but hopeful the future would be better.

The markets were higher than a year ago, in fact – much higher; yet, the enthusiasm and celebration for moving forward was starting to stall. This July would be like watching a fireworks display in the rain.

We would be near the end of our first market correction since the lows of March 2009. Both the economic recovery and the investor psyche were fragile, still jumpy and anxious for some sense of certainty and security. Market corrections are the quick reversals of fortunes; they leave you thinking you should have done something. But it doesn't work that way.

Oil was still gushing from the broken well in the gulf, along with the realization that a new flow of regulations would soon be gushing from Washington. Unemployment remained stubbornly high at 9.5%. Consumers were cautious.

One-party rule had reached its limits as Democrats reached for ideological gains in social issues, even when the tide of debt and joblessness was rising and would be foremost on voters' minds. With a very fragile recovery stalled, the congressional midterm elections started growing in significance; providing fertile ground for the Tea Party movement to grow.

CHAPTER
19

June 30, 2010

DJIA: 9,870.30
S&P: 1,041.24

What Are You Looking at, Scarecrow?

Let me begin with this quote from the late Milton Friedman; "Our whole monetary system owes its existence to the mutual acceptance of what, from one point of view, is no more than a fiction." I wish the financial train wreck occurring in this country were simply fiction. It is not. It is quite real and we all know someone who has been or is being touched by the unwinding of excess in our economy. As a nation, we are recognizing the fundamental notion that excess debt will have long-term consequences for our children and grandchildren. Government debt, unlike personal household debt has the power to disrupt the "fiction" that is the perceived value of money. In *The Wizard of Oz*, the command was given to "pay no attention to the man behind the curtain," but the travelers did, and the story was forever changed.

As investors, we are looking behind the curtain, and our confidence has been shaken. Yesterday came the news that consumer confidence declined from 62.7% in May to 52.9% in June. It's no coincidence this occurred right along with the disjointed and piecemeal government response to BP's Deep Horizon well disaster in the Gulf of Mexico. I believe we are witnessing a defining moment for the Obama administration as the economy teeters between recovery and recession. Without a coherent economic plan, offered soon, the U.S. economy and the fragile recovery are in danger. The American people intuitively know this and obviously investors do as well, yet, what we are looking for are the wizards of Washington to come to the same realization.

With another significant decline yesterday in the equity markets and a flight to safety in government bonds, you have to stay very cautious. With short-term interest rates near zero, it is reactive to want to earn more; but, the return *of* principal is more important than the return *on* principal. Clearly, there is little direction for investors to feel confident about. But, if the recovery continues, we are seeing attractive values in many sectors. As corporate earnings start to be released in early July, the strong corporate balance sheets of many U.S. companies should bring some stability to a very nervous market.

July 7, 2010

DJIA: 9,743.72

S&P: 1,028.06

The Heat Is On

There appear to be more questions than answers, but what is crystal clear is the lack of confidence rolling through the financial markets. Confidence is the one key ingredient missing from a summer rally, and the lack of confidence, I suspect, plays a significant role in the overall mood of the nation. Unemployment continues to be the chronic malady of the recovery. The prescription of massive amounts of government spending has had marginal effectiveness in relieving the employment crisis that continues to grow under the care of the current policy creators. Every day that passes makes it more apparent that our current economic leadership is lost in the wilderness. That doesn't build confidence, and the growing sense that the job of turning our economy around is too big a problem for academic policymakers is leading many market participants to wait out the next few months and the potential of an economic course correction from the midterm elections. The heat is definitely on for the Obama administration, but as we learn the White House will sue Arizona over immigration, you can't help but wonder if this isn't an act of fiddling as the nation burns.

Speaking of the midterm elections, you should probably know that there have been 28 midterm elections since 1898. In looking at June 30 to June 30 of those periods, it has been determined that the Dow Jones increased an average of 12.65% in 19 of the 28 time periods. In more recent history, in the 10 midterm elections since 1970 only one was negative; that was 2002 and the Dow lost 2.79%. I share this historical perspective not to predict the market, but rather to suggest something significant usually derives from the midterm elections. The largest increase was 1982; the market rose 50.5% and it coincides with a major shift from Keynesian economic policies of Jimmy Carter to massive tax cuts and supply-side policies of Ronald Reagan.

Next week begins another corporate earnings season, and we will see how the second quarter shaped up and we will have the opportunity to digest corporate outlooks for the balance of 2010. The market has preempted the fundamental case for higher stock prices and appears to have discounted many negatives that are reported daily in the media. The case for a double-dip recession seems more plausible today, however it is not clear if the fear of uncertainty and policy mistakes has created a bubble in Treasury bonds or our financial markets have become the barometer of bad news to come, and the flight to safety is the only move to make. In my 28-year career, I can say that the current environment is as difficult to predict as any time I have seen and experienced. The tensions that seem to build daily may reach a crescendo sometime before November, and I suspect the opportunities will become clearer. In the short term I must remain cautious, but with cash on the sidelines I'm building a "buy" list.

July 14, 2010

DJIA: 10,363.02
S&P: 1,095.34

A Blind Squirrel

Two weeks ago, with a high degree of pessimism in the markets I said; "But, if the recovery continues we are seeing attractive values in many sectors. As corporate earnings start to be released in early July, the strong corporate balance sheets of many U.S. companies should bring some stability to a very nervous market." Well, as the saying goes, "Even a blind squirrel finds a nut occasionally," and with a six-day rally in the markets, corporate earnings seems to be the catalyst. Do I think we have the all-clear sign for investors to become aggressive buyers? No, not really. My best guess is that our markets got very oversold and too pessimistic, and the uncertainty and volatility can play the market up as well as down.

I know I sound like a broken record, but I believe the midterm elections are acting like a ceiling for the next leg up of a bull market rally. The uncertainty I have been writing about is still with us and will most likely remain with us for the balance of 2010. If you are nervous, consider taking some profits. On the other hand, we are seeing some attractive values in companies with stellar balance sheets, and over the long run buying good blue chip stocks with dividends that pay higher returns than the 10-year Treasury bond is too good to not consider. Let the market volatility work for you, and, if suitable, put in an order to buy below the market and be patient.

Lastly, although I have been critical of the current administration's economic policies I want to welcome President Obama to Holland for the LG Battery plant groundbreaking ceremony. It's not every day the President visits your community, and certainly I hope his short time in Holland is memorable and uplifting. Actually, I hope a little West Michigan entrepreneurship rubs off on him and he decides to extend the Bush tax cuts; now that would be a "nut" worth finding.

July 21, 2010

DJIA: 10,229.96
S&P: 1,083.48

Lines Are Currently Busy

There appears to be a significant number of financial disconnects as I look at economic data today. When I look at the U.S. Treasury bond market, the very low historical interest rates seem to be signaling a significant slowdown in the U.S. economy on the horizon. When I look at the S&P 500 stock index, I see a market trading at relatively fair prices and good earnings reports continue to be released for the second quarter, which suggests the U.S. economy is growing, albeit slowly. In time, we will know whether the bond market has been a good barometer of a future recession and continued deflationary pressures or whether the Treasury bond market will become the next bubble, as money is simply chasing "risk free" returns at unprecedented levels. I lean toward a bubble growing in the bond market, especially given the reported $1.8 trillion that is sitting on corporate balance sheets looking for a home.

Another disconnect is showing up in the energy market as the oil-to-gas price ratio has ballooned to more than 20:1 from a historical ratio of 6:1 to 10:1. Again, the historic ratio would suggest oil should be $40 a barrel or natural gas should be $9

MMBtu, or double its current price. This is where a significant slowdown in the economy suggests $40 oil, yet we know yesterday Goldman Sachs raised its 12-month price target for crude oil to $100. The other possibility is that the new normal for the oil-to-gas ratio is 20:1. In time, we will know.

So the phrase "in time, we will know" continues to be the predominant theme for investors. The political forces rather than fundamental forces seem to be the key ingredient as to why we are seeing so many in-congruencies in our financial markets. At some point, investors willing to look out on the horizon with optimism will exploit the conflicting news and will capitalize on the inefficiencies of current events. I suspect they will buy stocks when no one else will; they will buy real estate when the fear of foreclosure is heightened and they will continue to buy their straw hats in the winter. Investors do that, it's in their DNA. So, be a patient investor, and let the markets come to you.

July 28, 2010

DJIA: 10,537.69
S&P: 1,113.84

"Leaving On a Jet Plane"

It's rare these days, quite rare, to discover a pattern or trend in the daily energy of our financial markets. Yet, we try; looking for that morsel of value, like the grizzled miner panning for flakes of gold. Slowly, day after day, our efforts leave us weary and frustrated; yet, the few flakes of gold are the constant reminders of the hope and promise of better days. For much of this year, the U.S. stock market has been the enigma, rather than the scoreboard, reflecting a vibrant and healthy corporate America. The trend is elusive; almost a foreign language or more of a riddle to solve than a reward for success. Salary and earnings are supposed to decide the rank of one's status, wise management is supposed to tell all, and sterling balance sheets are supposed to be the fruit of a blue chip pedigree. Investors crave such value, such stability, and yet, it's the peace of mind that is ultimately the unsaid reality of the matter. That's what's missing today, peace of mind. Investor contentment has become the antique in the corner, the embellished story told by a grandparent, or increasingly, it's the longing that investors can sense, but can never quite hold on to.

Though you resist, it is hard not to feel the daily pulling away of the retail investor. Like the miner who packs up his pick and supplies and moves on to weigh and cash in his meager flakes of gold, investors have worked their claims and are heading home. History is clear at this point, when the perception of stocks becomes far too risky we move to the comfort and safety of the familiar and simple life. Trillions of dollars have moved to the known and simple, under-productive and under-achieving, yielding just a few flakes of gold for months and months of panning. It's a melancholy moment for the American investor, a time of reminiscing on better days and a constant worry and fear that our best days are long gone. I wonder, are these times different? Are the markets just a reflection of the computers and soulless algorithms that tilt the scales with a heavy thumb?

History is sometimes the voice in the wilderness; lost in the urgency, in the volatility and the unpredictability of market movements. But, when the noise subsides we will hear the miner saying, "There's gold in them there hills," and the rush from cash to stocks will leave you breathless. So, as the song goes, you may have packed your bags and you're ready to go, but fight that urge and stay firm in your plan. Patiently wait; for the tide will usually turn, and I suspect there is a reward for those who persevere. Peace of mind is very valuable, and some might say invaluable, but a well-diversified portfolio provides investors the confidence to give these days time. Time to ride the storms of life and the volatility we are experiencing.

August 4, 2010

DJIA: 10,636.38
S&P: 1,120.46

Truth or Dare

Like the birthday party game truth or dare, each day economic and corporate data are given to investors, and each day investors have to tell the truth or take the dare. Recently the truth is that corporate earnings have unfolded better than anticipated - meanwhile, the dare that entails investors' buying common stock has been beyond nerve-wracking, as the proverbial wall of worry is formidable. I think investors realize that what may seemingly appear to be a daily media game of cat and mouse is really quite serious business when retirement savings and college funds hang and dangle in the balance.

At current levels, we are once again found in a place where we are afraid to be in the market, but also afraid to be out of it. The truth-or-dare aspect steps in and admittedly refreshes the priorities of the market, which reassures us that confidence prevails. Many investors continue to sit on the sidelines and tell the truth - they're scared - rather than approach the dare of believing that the markets will press on.

Like mentioned last week, the primary forces that would continue to push through this summer rally are pro-growth and pro-business public policy. Alongside that is the incentive to put cash to work. With such policies, the future of capital sits idly, waiting for a more certain and stable environment. With $1.8 trillion in corporate money on the sidelines, the current circumstances are desperately seeking attention.

So, for investors, it's truth or dare time.

In the summer of 2010, politics, rather than economics, seemed to dominate the news. Politics brings a rare dynamic to the daily trading of the dog days of summer – mostly a symptom of a lack of interest as volume tends to slow down. For most of the summer, the markets were locked into a very tight trading range, with little economic energy to move the needle.

Nearly half of the states hold primary elections in August and September; all with an eye on the November midterm elections. With little energy in the markets, the passion of primary voters was obvious. From the emergence of the Tea Party to the nervous bravado of House Speaker Nancy Pelosi, the primary season was the warm-up act for what was to come in November.

In my case, I was intimately involved as an insider for a gubernatorial primary in the state of Michigan. Pete Hoekstra was an 18-year veteran of Congress and had represented the Second Congressional District in the conservative fashion that was the essence of the district. As a candidate for governor, you visit many small towns and attend county fairs and ethnic festivals; all told you travel thousands of miles and hear thousands of stories.

I was treasurer of the campaign, and as a personal friend of the candidate, I took the time and opportunity to visit with people from around the state. I learned that people in Tawas or Frankenmuth had similar concerns to those of people in Cheboygan or Manistee. When traveling from Midland to Mount Pleasant and on to Lake City, you saw the same John Deere tractors beside the barns. I noticed the majestic views of Mackinac Island and the abundant natural resources you see for miles and miles.

I saw oil wells and wind farms, farms of corn and farms of eggs; I saw a rural part of Michigan that seemed so normal. Yet, I also saw the broken soul of the auto industry traveling through Saginaw, Flint and ending in Detroit. There was a soberness to a once great city, humbled by the force of the economic malaise.

I would listen to the people at the rallies; I would hear their stories and their wishes for change. Isn't every election about change? But, I could see in their eyes a desperation born of not being heard. It's interesting to me that in a state where billions poured in from Washington to rescue GM and Chrysler, people wanted to talk about Ford; and there was a certain pride in their voices as they would say, "They didn't need government." Just one more clue of what was coming in November.

Like I said, politics brings a rare dynamic and when you approach election day there is a growing pressure. That's urgency, a word missing from behind the fortress walls of Washington – just one more disconnect from the soul of Main Street.

We would lose the election, but I gained a fresh fondness for my state and the everyday people who embrace hard work, family and faith. I was a better American after that summer. I learned how important it was to listen, how easy it is to get distracted from the real issues of the day and how important it is to understand that our financial markets are just a small part of what is the strength of so many communities.

Labor Day was just around the corner. Maybe it was fitting to be in Michigan reminiscing about my summer adventure.

CHAPTER
20

August 11, 2010

DJIA: 10,644.25

S&P: 1,121.06

Where Are All of the Adults?

There were no surprises when the Federal Reserve maintained its interest rate policy yesterday. Clearly, evidence is mounting that the economic recovery that began in March of 2009 has been historically anemic and is losing steam, as jobless claims continue to bewitch the administration and the Keynesian policies it has pursued. After selling off early in the day, markets rallied on the news, leaving observers somewhat confused over the next move. Personally, I find myself believing that there is a "greater something" that is overlooked as I decipher the enigma we call the market. I hear experts talk about deflation, yet I am more concerned about inflation. Believe it or not, I heard the phrase "noflation" yesterday, and I'm pretty sure it means "I don't know what's going to happen with GDP, interest rates and prices, and I certainly don't know what the markets will do next." Noflation. Maybe that's a Wall Street term for "frustration"....OK, maybe I made that up.

As you have probably guessed, I like to read; especially opinions and editorials that make you think and feel. The following quote by Peggy Noonan of the *Wall Street Journal* captured my attention this week, illuminating a growing perception that many investors seem to share. Perhaps it reveals that "greater something" that is missing;

"When the adults of a great nation feel long-term pessimism, it only makes matters worse when those in authority take actions that reveal their detachment from the concerns - even from the essential nature - of their fellow citizens. And it makes those citizens feel powerless."

There is a word that was prominent in the 1970s that rolls long-term pessimism and detachment in to one phrase; that word is "malaise." Like observing a slow-motion train wreck, we feel helpless, hopeless, and sad at the inevitable outcome. The problem is, here in 2010 we have seen this train before and we are failing to heed its warning. By the end of 1979, the national malaise created an inflationary environment that brought about an austerity plan of high interest rates to break the back of inflation. We have experienced only two double-dip recessions in the past 100 years; both times they were caused by external forces of public policy. In the case of the last double-dip, then-Fed Chairman Paul Volker hiked interest rates to curb inflation, which unfolded into the recession of 1982. Are we headed for the third double-dip recession caused by an external force? With public policy adjustments encouraging production and investment, it would be unlikely. In the event that policy makers remain on the current course, it is reasonable to conclude that an external force will be thrown at the economy as the current lackluster performance carries on.

One last point to make; it is easy to feel doom and gloom, but, when it comes to stock prices, you need to keep in mind the fundamental value of an enterprise and its comparable value to other investments. The market seems poised for a higher move. Despite the tyranny of uncertainty and a somewhat hostile business environment, we are witnessing creative people finding ways to be profitable. Don't give up on this market just yet, but understand if we see higher taxes, growing deficits, slowing employment, and GDP growth under 2%, then risk-taking will most likely not be rewarded. The midterm elections will give us a good look at future policy moves.

Near the end of August, I put in my journal a reflection on my weariness of a long summer. My intent was to send it to my clients. But I didn't, and I really can't say why. I make a practice of waiting a few days before I send a more personal missive to friends and clients, but shortly after I wrote this, the markets would begin a massive rally, one that would last well into 2011.

Here, is what I almost said:

I enjoy reading, and I especially like to read journalists and editorials that make you think and feel. Two quotes captured my attention this week, revealing a growing perception many investors seem to share. I try to filter partisan talking points from both sides, as my experience has taught me stock prices are deaf to the cacophony of self-proclaimed truth-tellers of special interests and the media, but stock prices do respond to our national psyche and behaviors, even as the media report on the symptoms. Here are the quotes.

"Expanding bureaucracies and government control of industries and economic sectors are antithetical to the principles of free enterprise that foster industry and opportunity. They put our economic future at risk."

"When the adults of a great nation feel long-term pessimism, it only makes matters worse when those in authority take actions that reveal their detachment from the concerns – even from the essential nature – of their fellow citizens. And it makes those citizens feel powerless."

Two themes, "economic future at risk" and "citizens feel powerless" seem to converge, creating an atmosphere in which investors are simply fearful – scared for their future, their children, their retirements, and, most of all, a growing and persistent unease the world is spinning out of control. In my long career, I have never had more clients say to me that they are scared for America than in the past 18 months. Yet, as I look at history, I see example after example of why fear can be justified. Usually, it was caused by an enemy who wished to do America harm. We found our courage and defeated our enemies, again and again.

Today, it's different. The growing unease is from the perceived enemy within our borders, right and left, and the casualties caused by "friendly fire" are the most disheartening. With dismal employment reports, we see the economic battlefield strewn with weary participants fighting for control of the American dream.

I wonder – I truly wonder – if come November, we won't witness a second Gettysburg. Intuitively, we feel and understand the divide that has spread across our nation. Investors and corporations alike have moved to the sidelines of the embattled marketplace and wait for the smoke to clear. Gettysburg was the worst experience in the lives of many Americans, north and south, and yet, it was the turning point for what would become the best of America. How weary and confused were the American people in early July of 1863?

Here is my point: The markets tend to respond well in advance of the battle's outcome. Similar to the family pet foretelling a destructive earthquake, the financial markets tend to sense the trend to come. Now, I don't know the final outcome for November, for our cultural divide is deep and wide, but I do know the amount of cash waiting and wanting to be productive is massive, and, if unleashed from the tyranny of uncertainty, a bull market will charge ahead.

Fast fact: There have been only two double-dip recessions in the past 100 years; 1937 and 1982. Both times, external shocks and bad public policies appear to have caused the double-dip.

CHAPTER
21

August 18, 2010

DJIA: 10,405.85
S&P: 1,092.54

View From the Shade

Like the summer haze that reminds us of hot and humid weather, the dog days of August have settled upon us. Life murmurs to a standstill, and it takes more effort to work through the heat of the moment. For investors, the grind of this last month of summer has forced us into the shade. We watch as the volatility that has defined this crisis continues to push and pull prices to extremes, and yet we're comfortable in the shade simply watching the drama of Wall Street unravel. Increasingly, we are seeing technology play a more profound role in the daily behavior of the many markets we follow. With individual and corporate investors on the sidelines, we are seeing computer-programmed trading employ an increasing daily influence of stock, bond, and commodity prices. Will this have a long-term impact? Ask me in September. That sounds so far away as we sit and relax in the shade, but weeks from now summer will be over and the rush to the midterm elections and end of the year will be in full motion.

This week's comments by Raymond James chief investment strategist Jeff Saut puts into perspective the confusion professional money managers are having as they attempt to weather the after-effects of the financial crisis. With more instability, we seek strategies that provide greater flexibility; this is a distinct difference from the strategies of the '80s and '90s, which were "buy and hold"-dominated times. But, looking even further into the market dynamics, you start to notice asset groups trading together that historically would not have. For example, the price of oil and the S&P 500 stock index are trading alongside one another, when, in ordinary circumstances, they would not have, or at least not quite to this extreme. In other words, diversification, as opposed to asset class, is not having the calming effect for your portfolio that history would suggest. I'm not suggesting you stop diversifying, I am simply suggesting you have to be more patient in allowing a balanced portfolio to work for you.

Well, it's mid-August and my Chicago Cubs are 20 games below .500. The summer rally has lost some steam, but despite all of the reasons to be cautious on the market, I remain vigilantly optimistic as we complete this year. As for my Cubs; "wait until next year"!

August 25, 2010   DJIA: 10,041.45
                                   S&P: 1,051.87

The Story You Are About to See Is...

As we wind down the summer, the camper will be folded up,
picnic baskets put away for the season, and all of the sports
camps finally end and parents welcome the beginning of school.
Perhaps this fits you; or really this summer has been difficult
for many reasons and a new day would just be welcomed. I don't
know your personal circumstance, but I want to reflect on
life. The financial crisis that began in 2008 continues to
reverberate and craft the new face of America. My partners
here at Zichterman & Clark have been questioning my comments
after the past couple of weeks as to what am I really trying
to say; and maybe that's a fair question, maybe you share that
sentiment. Well, let me attempt to assure my partners there is
a core to my story-telling and analogies and at the end of the
day, perhaps you will let my thoughts marinate and help give
directions for your goals and objectives. So, as detective Joe
Friday from the old television show *Dragnet* supposedly said,
"Just the facts ma'am," here we go.

We continue to be in the midst of the financial crisis that
began with the collapse of Bear Stearns in March of 2008.
Investors, and when I say investors I mean individuals like
you and me, have experienced a psychological trauma that is
fading, but will continue to shape our behaviors, much like our
parents and grandparents were shaped by the Great Depression.
It has been a defining moment that our culture has phrased the
new normal. This has been like a piece of art, and when you
look at a piece of art, you have a personal opinion as to the

quality of the work. For two years, the effects of our economy and markets have left us with our uniquely personal perspective.

We are in a financial crisis that has partisan politics intertwined and woven in to so many levels that it has created an environment of uncertainty that has rarely been experienced in American history. It is my opinion that the current economic agenda has hit the proverbial ideological dead end, and without a significant policy pivot, a self-fulfilling prophecy of a double-dip recession could occur. The financial crisis will not conclude without true courage of leadership and implementing policies that empower the private sector to once again embrace the American Dream and create jobs to make profits and give back to their local communities. The American Dream is not perfect, and too many Americans were falling behind, but I ask; "If not the American Dream, what dream would it be?"

This market has been range-bound for most of this year, and I find it difficult to describe in fresh ways why we keep bouncing from highs to lows. I'm running out of analogies, but here's my view: Come November, as a nation, we will come to a philosophical fork in the road. Like that piece of art, I will let you envision what those choices are. However, a choice will be made, and for now hedging your bets has been the prudent course. Finally, I still leave you with these words: Don't despair. I believe in America and the collective wisdom of its people. History has shown, and at this critical junction in American history, the seeds of recovery are on the sidelines waiting for clarity and renewed fertile soil.

September 1, 2010   DJIA: 10,014.72
                      S&P: 1,049.33

The More Things Change...

"The U.S. economy remains almost comatose. The slump already ranks as the longest period of sustained weakness since the Depression. The economy is staggering under many 'structural' burdens, as opposed to familiar 'cyclical' problems. The structural faults represent once-in-a-lifetime dislocations that will take years to work out. Among them: the job drought, the debt hangover, the banking collapse, the real estate depression, the health care cost explosion, and the runaway federal deficit." *Time* magazine, 1992

Perspective is everything in today's markets. Perhaps you remember 1992 and the broad weakness of the U.S. economy and the S&L crisis of the time. I stumbled upon this quote from *Time* earlier this week and felt it was instructive to the overly pessimistic aura of our economy's current situation. The contrarian in me believes the market appears to be littered with good values. What many times may have seemed as too-high of a wall to climb, in retrospect, was not. Though it's nearly two decades later, is it really any different this time? Is it merely a situation in which the knot is just tied too tightly to undo? I remind you that we have a $14 trillion economy as measured by GDP, a number that has nearly doubled since 1992. In over 10 years, we should see more than $140 trillion worth of economic activity; that's an amount of money where a change of even 1% or 2% can be a substantial shift of our fiscal trajectory. If we see inflation, which we should expect to occur, that number could be much higher and the debt crisis would appear more manageable. By the way, U.S. GDP was $7.4 trillion in 1992.

http://www.data360.org/dsg.aspx?Data_Set_Group_Id=230

Let me be clear, the problems we face will take significant political cooperation, which is sadly missing today. It is quite easy to lose track of the economy's present condition as it compares in totality of the overall history of our economy, so you have to remind yourself, and your confidence in the market, that what we are experiencing right now is unprecedented. While looking at our current situation, we often forget that we've been here before. As Mark Twain once said, "History doesn't repeat itself, it simply rhymes."

September 8, 2010

DJIA: 10,340.69
S&P: 1,091.84

Don't Give Up

USA Today on Thursday, September 2, presented us with an investor-prophetic moment not to be forgotten. The headline from the Money section reads, "Shell-shocked investors quit the market: Could dizzying losses create a 1930s-style lost generation?" http://bit.ly/cX1A5o

It is simply uncanny how magazine covers, newspapers, or the nightly news have a way of stating the obvious... after the fact. Not only after the fact, but they also provide a clue to an unseen shift in sentiment that has not been reported or detected by a journalist contrary to their article's premise. Consumer and investor psyches have certain mysticism when trying to reason their behavior. History has shown that the media are looking in the rearview mirror and have a way of calling a market top or bottom by reporting just the opposite. I would suggest with the headline above that there is now a very real possibility that investors will start finding ways to invest that cash.

To be fair, Adam Shell of USA Today has put his finger on the raw feelings of many investors. His description is accurate. The trauma many investors have experienced is very real, but it's his conclusion and premise I find instructive. Here is my belief: When the masses believe a market has only one direction, a herd mentality dominates and will take you to where you may not want to go. Much has been written about the psychology of crowds, and I ask you, how collectively thoughtful is a mob? The mob of conservative investors, disillusioned by the random volatility of our current markets, has become a very large crowd of risk-averse people. It is OK to be cautious and prudent; I'm not saying risk doesn't exist. I'm just advising not to let the crowd think for you; only you know your goals and objectives, and, ultimately, your risk tolerance.

Basketball coach and cancer victim Jim Valvano said it best in his moving and emotional speech at the ESPY awards in 1993. His quote and passion is what I would say to you: "Don't give up, don't ever give up." http://bit.ly/8wtrFt

Successful investing is hard work, and often you must persevere the uncertainty of the times. But, don't quit on America or the vital optimism of the belief that our best days are still before us. As Warren Buffet once said, "Be fearful when others are greedy; be greedy when others are fearful."

As a nation, it was sadly ironic that we would enter the Labor Day holiday with unemployment hovering at 9.5%. The five stages of grief seemed to be stretched out over two years, as our economy slowly was finding some solid ground. The final stage of grief is acceptance; in the fall of 2010, most people were resigned to a stubbornly high rate of unemployment. I also suspect that most Americans believed we were underachieving, and voters have a difficult time with that particular sin. Perhaps this point is instructive as we begin to look toward the 2012 presidential election.

As it turns out, this stretch of time would be the launching pad of the second leg of the bull market that began in March of 2009; the markets tend to be out ahead of our feelings and perceptions. Amazingly, despite the general melancholy of our national grieving, stocks turned up in anticipation of strong earnings to come.

There was this overarching debate economists were having, with no clear answer, but significant policy implications. Investors were being faced with a dilemma: Was our economy suffering from protracted deflationary forces or could we begin to concentrate on the inflationary pressures sure to arise?

My alma mater is Hope College in Holland, Michigan, snuggled along the shores of Lake Michigan and most famous for windmills and tulips; like many small college towns, we are rich in tradition.

One tradition is the picture of what investors were facing: "The Pull," a giant rope, two teams on opposite banks of the Black River, each dedicated in their quest to pull the other team into the river. It symbolized the tension between deflation and inflation. Investors would have to calibrate their portfolios to best encounter either deflation or inflation. I believed then that inflation would eventually pull the deflationists into the river. Currently, with $4 a gallon gasoline, I think I was right.

CHAPTER
22

September 15, 2010

DJIA: 10,526.49
S&P: 1,121.10

September 11, 2010
_____

While reflecting on 9/11, I have been consuming the intense media coverage of events nine years ago. Through this exposure, I have noticed that the emotional scars for investors are becoming more evident. Last week, we talked about the need to not give up and in turn, think about moving forward - which is easier said than done, as the assessment of risk cannot be easily ascertained. But, for the past nine years, the average investor has been the piece of driftwood in a vast ocean, an ocean that has been roiled by the winds of change and uncertainty.

We still seem to be searching for reconciliation between the cruel reality of modern terrorism and the hopes and dreams of a secure retirement. You want to move forward and you know you need to move forward, but that nagging feeling of looking over your shoulder continues to erode the confidence you once experienced. The media coverage of 9/11 is still fresh in my mind, and I hope I never forget the heroic moments that were shining stars in a very dark moment. We were proud to be Americans then, but now we seem confused as to what "American" means. The scars of defining moments have always been difficult for investors. Yet, investors are very resilient, and over time, one would suspect that a growing confidence will return and the vast sum of cash reserves should come back into the U.S. economy.

This ninth anniversary will come and go, and beyond the reverence of honoring the victims, I wonder if we will recognize how our national agenda was and continues to be held hostage to those events. Unlike the Iranian hostage crisis, our current crisis is internal in nature. Our swagger was lost on 9/11, along with that deep confidence in who we are as a nation and the belief in a better tomorrow. Though it was a tragedy, our country came together nine years ago to fight the hard times. I urge you to remember that prevailing through economic hard times or political uncertainties is an American value, a value that we should continue to have con-fidence in.

Maybe, everything in life is just one big chain reaction; every action results in a reaction, the push and pull, the yin and yang. After two years of experiencing first-hand a financial crisis that quite possibly has been on par with the Great Depression, we questioned the connection piece of the puzzle: Was there a balance? The world seemed more disconnected than connected, with the final consequence – the many extraordinary measures taken – remaining an open question.

The markets were performing remarkably well, anticipating better news in 2011 as the Dow Jones average broke through 11,000. For the casual observer, we were making progress. Of course, most investors still were clinging to cash, but felt better about their future.

The midterm elections were just around the corner, with early indications heavily favored toward a shift in public policy. Looking back, we know it would be a major shift and could be seen as a parliamentary type vote of no-confidence in the direction the country was heading.

This would be a seminal moment for the President as the arc of future policy priorities was diminished by the election results. However, for investors, we simply exchanged one set of uncertainties for another.

The subtle story running alongside the election was a major monetary experiment planned to be unleashed come the first of the year. Quantitative easing is a monetary tool used by the Federal Reserve. It is simply the act of buying debt securities issued by the U.S. Treasury in the marketplace with the stated objective of lowering long-term interest rates.

At the margin, QE (Quantitative Easing) can be a useful tool. However, the size and scope of the Federal Reserve's proposed QE plan was aggressive and would be considered an unprecedented experiment. Under this proposal, the Federal Reserve planned to buy up to $600 billion-worth of securities. I don't believe the average citizen fully comprehended or appreciated the potential risk and consequences inherent in this policy.

The creation of money and then the extraction of that newly created currency is a balancing act of economics and politics. The success or failure of this program will be something historians and economists will debate for years.

For some reason, I don't believe my grandchildren will appreciate the argument that had we not moved forward with QE2 (the second round of Quantitative Easing) it would have been worse.

CHAPTER
23

September 22, 2010
DJIA: 10,761.03
S&P: 1,139.78

The Play

You don't have to be a football fan to be able to appreciate the conclusion of the Michigan State-Notre Dame game that took place this past Saturday night. Sometimes, life does come down to a single play or moment and the outcome forever changes our view. There is a certain poetry to a well-executed trick play. A trick, because it was unexpected, unexpected from a coach and a team that have coveted the narrative of conservative. When looking at the U.S. economy, are we being lulled into the narrative of slow growth and deflation?

The National Bureau of Economic Research declared that the recession officially ended in June 2009, however, the consensus forecast for 2010 seems to be that the U.S. growth rate will be 2% or lower, with little economic strength to create much-needed jobs. But, I wonder if is there a trick play being set up for investors. Currently, the stock market has seen a very strong advance, a nearly 800-point climb against considerable headwinds. Common belief is the markets have come too far, too fast, to be sustained. Well...maybe?

I suspect an event not on the financial radar today will be "the play" for 2010. From retail sales to housing starts, from built-up inventory to foreign trade, the clouds of ambiguity reinforces the plot of slow growth, and the belief we have a deep hole to climb out of. So, it's the fourth quarter, the game could go either way, and perhaps the markets could be in for a reverse.

What if the government bureaucracies get out of the way and regulators stop playing in the game and instead start officiating the game? What if the U.S. entrepreneur breaks free from the ropes of uncertainty much like Gulliver awakening and being held captive by the Lilliputians to finally break free as a giant? Do we know the pent-up buying power of the U.S. consumer? There are a lot of what-ifs, but like any good trick play, it is in the misdirection and execution, which brings about the sudden impact, and in the words of our President, we could see a game-changer.

It's obvious the midterm elections will most likely have an impact on the markets. What's not obvious is the ultimate unleashing of the trillions of dollars waiting for just the right moment to be invested in growing businesses and hiring people. Now that's a trick play we all would like to see.

September 29, 2010 · DJIA: 10,858.14
S&P: 1,147.70

Hop On This Bus

What is it about a children's song that simply cuts to the obvious? These words and melody kept playing in my head as I traveled the other day.

"The wheels on the bus go round and round, / round and round, / round and round. / The wheels on the bus go round and round, / all through the town."

What I observed were not buses, but rather the big heavy rigs of our nation's biggest corporations and transportation companies. It made me wonder about the current rally on Wall Street and whether the Dow Jones Transportation Average Index has been participating. Since the beginning of September, that index has risen more than 12%. It is hard to imagine the U.S. economy recovering without the transportation index signaling better days ahead. I think this index, much like the overall market, signals an improved economy about six to nine months from now. This current rally has been stronger and more durable than most would have expected. With a few more positive days, this September could be the best September since 1939.

But, hold on...a report out Tuesday morning shows consumers turned decidedly pessimistic in September. The Conference Board's index of consumer confidence fell to 48.5 this month from 53.2 in August. The September reading was far worse than the 52.0 expected by economists, and is the lowest reading since February 2010. The board said "worries about the labor markets are weighing on consumers." In August, investors were decidedly pessimistic, and now consumer confidence is reported in recession-like levels. We wonder: Why all the uncertainty? It's the conflicting messages we seem to get daily that has confounded the average investor.

With the midterm elections a little more than a month away, it would appear the markets are feeling more comfortable with where the economy will be in 2011. Is that a result of sweeping changes potentially in Congress or simply the ratcheting down of the many uncertainties that U.S. businesses have been plagued with for much of 2010? We can't be certain. But the anecdotal evidence I continue to observe is that perhaps the Great Recession is coming to a close and a new beginning is under way. I notice the mall parking lots with more cars now than 18 months ago, the daily traffic on the roads simply going to lunch, and of course the number of trucks, yes, those big ones carrying everything imaginable. The next time you're out, notice...notice the activity, watch consumers going about their days and then remember what makes up an economy. It's people, interacting with people, buying goods and services. By just observing, we may notice we are closer to a sustained recovery than we realize. I think the massive deleveraging of speculation and debt is winding down, and a more reasonable rhythm of economic activity is slowly developing. That being the case, the markets are simply reflecting what I discern...the wheels on the trucks go round and round, all through the town.

Our world seems to be changing too quickly to understand "precedent" as a word that suggests something old, stodgy and irrelevant, instead of something tried and true. Cultural shifts occur at such an accelerated pace we are challenged to know at any point in time where the collective mood of the nation resides. In our modern world, with the Internet and social media, so much information is now available that the most engaging and compelling voice wins.

In the 2008 presidential election, Barack Obama had the most compelling voice and the most engaging message. By November of 2010 the voice had been silenced and the message vanished. As quickly as you can change your status on Facebook, the national attention shifted: We "like" this and we click the button. For Republicans, the November elections would be the voting public giving a:

The midterm elections would be a seismic shift of power, something rarely seen in American history. I was stunned by the momentum swing in just two years. The frustration was obvious, the rebuke was clear, and yet, the real message I took away from November would be the growing tide of independent voices – voters who wouldn't claim a team, but loved the game and their country, would simply go to the polls to make a difference.

Meanwhile, back on Wall Street, money had been waiting, preparing for a better time to take a risk. The midterm election provided the needed stimulus to help move paralyzed investors into the market. The rally, which began around Labor Day, would continue, lasting well into the spring of 2011 and producing a massive run of more than 2,800 points on the Dow Jones average.

The midterm elections provided relief from the cultural crusade that had been waged against the "middle right" majority, holding hostage millions of investors. The stars were now aligned for a rally, and that is exactly what happened.

October 6, 2010

DJIA: 10,944.72

S&P: 1,160.75

Surf's Up

It takes roughly 3% GDP growth to add net jobs to the U.S. economy; in golfing terms, that is par. A bogey would be less than that, and when you look back one month ago at the revision of second-quarter GDP to 1.6%, you realize, perhaps as a nation, that we experienced a double bogey and the next hole is looking rather difficult, with water on the right and the green surrounded by traps. For you non-golfers - let's just say that difficult issues lie ahead. In economic terms, stubborn high unemployment and lagging GDP growth leads one to believe in a deflation theme. Unlike a round of golf, the anemic economic recovery and jobs outlook is worrisome and serious. So, let's unpack what deflation is and why you may want to care.

Deflation is usually brought about by a lack of consumer and corporate demand on goods and services, resulting in falling prices. With trillions of dollars sitting on the sidelines and consumers saving and not spending, clearly there has been a lack of demand for goods and services in the private sector. The question for investors is: Will this be a long-term phenomenon like the lost decade in Japan? I want to paint a word-picture to describe the economic theme we think best describes our times. Before I do, I add this disclaimer: The risk inherent in the short run may not be the obvious risk in the long run. In other words, when you are drowning, don't mistake the shark for a life preserver. When you are drowning in uncertainty, the natural reflex is to reach for Treasuries, and right now I would caution you to consider the inflation risk of that Treasury. Rising rates creates falling bond prices; will interest rates be higher or lower in the future?

Here is the economic word-picture I see unfolding, and it's best described as a financial tsunami. In the beginning stages of a tsunami, the water recedes and the problems it creates seem quite serious. I would suggest this represents the deflationary pressures we are currently experiencing. My house-boat tied to the dock is sitting on the beach, my waterfront property is no longer on the water and I'm realizing my water economy has deflated, so to speak. The risk of withdrawing water is real, but moving to high ground instead of closer to shore seems overly cautious, after all we may simply have more beach. But, in the case of a tsunami, after being displaced the water returns with a much stronger force than when it receded. I would suggest the creation of money by the Federal Reserve could create a wave of inflation, which rebounds the deflationary forces we see today. For investors, higher ground looks different from the beach. In this case, high ground could be owning common stock. My fear is that the beach is littered with Treasury bonds, bonds that won't hold up when the wave comes in.

We may already be seeing the signs of inflation or re-inflation as the Dow Jones average approaches 11,000 and an overall spike in commodity prices - especially gold, which historically has been a harbinger of rising prices. The stock market continues to show signs of strong momentum and a general sense of unease, at times even a bit stronger than expected. In rising markets we call this the proverbial wall of worry, and unless the monetary policy of the Federal Reserve becomes less accommodative, I would continue to believe in this rally. Be on the lookout for a jobs report today and again on Friday morning.

October 13, 2010

DJIA: 11,020.40
S&P: 1,169.77

Money Mischief

It's confusing whether the Federal Reserve is a branch of government or a private enterprise, but what has usually been the case is a phrase I have used, "Don't fight the Fed." What do we mean by that? Currently, the Federal Reserve has been involved with and talking about expanding a monetary tool referred to as quantitative easing. Simply, the Federal Reserve is expanding the money supply by purchasing bonds and mortgages from financial institutions, in effect, growing the money supply and allowing for more liquidity in the system and expanding credit. Financial assets tend to rise when you have a Federal Reserve that is seen as accommodative. Clearly, when you create money, or in effect print money, you are accommodative.

This has helped to create a market with very strong momentum behind it, reaching the milestone of 11,000 on the Dow Jones average. What has been interesting is that the sell-offs early in the day seem to dissipate by the afternoon, leaving the market positive. That is a clear sign of a healthy rally. If I could put this current rally into baseball terms, I would say we are in the seventh inning and it's time to sing "Take Me Out to the Ball Game."

Whenever the markets have a move-up of more than 1,000 points I get a little nervous, but with a few innings to go before the midterm elections, I see enough momentum to carry this rally a bit further.

The rally began at the beginning of September, and as I mentioned back then, we had an environment of extreme pessimism. Refer back to the USA Today article that I highlighted on September 8th that ran the headline "Shell-shocked investors quit the market." Oftentimes, headlines of extreme pessimism or optimism can be turning points in the markets. This rally probably will not end until you see a headline claiming a new bull market has begun and it's safe to enter the market. I don't know when that will be, but for now money is moving from the sidelines to the market and despite the political season we are in investors are focused on something else. Time may be just what we need as we look out into 2011.

October 20, 2010

DJIA: 10,978.62

S&P: 1,165.90

The Quiet Risks

You can't ignore a sell-off in stocks when a sudden change occurs. Unfortunately, these abrupt adjustments to the market's main trend have been the new normal for investors. Yesterday was no exception as the momentum shifted from higher prices to a more cautious outlook. America has reached the stage in the current rally where it is hard to see how stocks can go much higher without new fundamental data to support these prices. Yesterday, we simply took profits. Hallelujah?

It's interesting to me that much like the crash of 2008, which evolved in the mortgage market, it was the news of mortgage-backed securities and Bank of America that gave the negative push to the market sell-off. Will this be the beginning of another credit crisis for U.S. banks? It might be too early to tell. Keep in mind how it is becoming increasingly more difficult to discern fact from fiction now that we are merely two weeks away from the midterm elections - the airwaves are flooded with political ads, the kind that frankly require suspending reality to believe most of their propagandist claims. I suspect the next two weeks will be filled with political noise and a market that takes a needed pause as we allow the earnings season to signal economic improvement for next year.

Moving forward, there are risks on the radar that the media have ignored, and, consequently, investors aren't thinking about. The mortgage issue and Chinese interest rate increase make for good news, but I don't believe these are the real issues to fret about. Here are the three issues catching my concern presently:

Protection in our currency and trade. With a strong populist atmosphere here in the U.S., it doesn't take much to move toward protectionist policies. An all-out trade war or currency war would be counter-productive to the world economic growth. Yet, Brazil is now taxing foreign investment into their government debt, which could be seen as a pre-emptive protectionist move.

The Eurozone. The Eurozone still holds unhealthy debt problems, which could lead to what I call Eurozone 2.0, as weak members are removed from the euro and the world is faced with a "New Europe". Uncertainty over the weak nations such as Greece could be a trigger of a currency war. Which countries are in; which are out?

Public policy shift. Lastly, will we see a shift in the U.S. public policy to represent values that are intrinsically a little more pro-business, pro-employment, pro-*growth*? A policy change might encourage employment, or will our current trajectory keep us on a gliding path facing headwinds toward European levels of unemployment?

These three items are not exhaustive of the issues we face, but I do believe they have the ability to alter the current market and its outlook. These are high risks that are unacknowledged and under-reported right now. The current rally is looking a little tired. But, any major pull-back in prices would be more of a buying opportunity, rather than beginning a new bear market.

October 27, 2010

DJIA: 11,169.46
S&P: 1,185.64

Death Cross vs. Gold Cross

Here is the headline from the Monday's Wall Street Journal; " 'X' Marks Spot - as Stocks Rise." Like finding a treasure map, looking for pirated gold, our long-lost adventure is highlighted by "X marks the spot." How simple is that? The one good thing that has come out of the economic turmoil of the past two years has been the colorful lingo of Wall Street. Recently, a technical indicator for the S&P 500 revealed the revered "gold cross." This comes a few months after we were exposed to the "death cross." These are heavy and ominous phrases, but let's break down what they really mean.

In both cases, we are referring to the moving averages of the market. In this case, looking at the 50-day moving average and the 200-day moving average, their intersection reveals the conditions of the cross. When the 50-day moving average moves down through the 200-day moving average, you have the dreaded death cross. Likewise, when that 50-day moving average breaks above the 200-day average, you have the coveted gold cross. Most of us simply want to retire someday and not run out of money, and now you find out you must worry about a death cross and not miss the gold cross. I think sometimes we just get too deep in the weeds when all you really need to know is whether the outlook for corporate earnings and interest rates is favorable. One indicator rarely tells the whole story, but can still create a remarkable conspiracy.

For traders of the markets, short-term indicators can be useful, helpful and sometimes accurate in turning a profit. We have talked about momentum and how the individual investor has been on the sidelines; this leaves a technical and institutional market reading the charts. But, we are one week from the election, which could bring the current agenda to an end and possibly bring some needed clarity or create even more uncertainty. Here is what I will say about the weeks ahead of us; as I read the tea leaves: This market is getting a little frothy. It would not surprise me to see the election bring about a correction for stocks. If that were to happen, given an election outcome that most expect—Republicans retake the House—my advice would be to buy stocks on weakness. Last week we talked about the risks in the markets, but the real political story isn't what is taking place just in Washington. When you pick up the paper on Wednesday, the real story is what happened not just in Washington, but the state and local elections. As far as we know, the 2012 presidential election begins next Wednesday.

November 3, 2010

DJIA: 11,188.72
S&P: 1,193.57

Reboot

Two major events will guide the markets in the weeks and months ahead. First, the midterm elections are behind us and the ultimate outcome was widely expected. Second, the Federal Reserve will announce this afternoon the expected size of QE2, otherwise known as quantitative easing 2. Both of these events have profound implications for our economy and perhaps will encourage the corporate cash that has been idle to begin to invest in expansion.

First, the midterm election. My take is once again we seem to have experienced an unprecedented event. Certainly, this will be seen as a Republican victory, but upon further review it is the independent voter who may be able to claim victory. What is significant is that, like our financial markets, the independent voter has added political unpredictability to the mix as we start to look at the 2012 presidential election. It appears as though we had many split tickets, which suggests non-party-affiliated voters are looking for people to solve problems, rather than voting out of loyalty. This could be a force to break political gridlock as politicians have learned there are consequences for their votes.

QE2 will be another massive infusion of money into the economy. This could help put idle money to work, as buying bonds by the Federal Reserve should push interest rates and the cost of borrowing lower. The risk of this is printing money, and inflation could be the ultimate effect of this action. Consider this morning that India and Australia are raising interest rates to slow inflation expectations in their economies. This could be bad news for the U.S. dollar and strengthen commodity prices.

The markets continue to look slightly over-bought here, which is to say a normal correction or pause would seem likely. But, and this is a big but, these are not normal times. Corporations are anxious to move forward, investors are anxious to move forward, and the average U.S. citizen is also ready to move forward. In other words, the wave of pessimism that has dampened our collective psyche just may be seeing the sunshine. After two years of a deep cultural divide that caused heightened anxieties and monumental uncertainty, average Americans and businesspeople just want to move on and make a better life for themselves and their families. We can agree to disagree on policies, but we should never discount the drive and entrepreneurial spirit of the American people.

Today's market, and maybe the balance of this week, will most likely signal if the rally can extend into the balance of this year. It's too early to know what policy changes may occur in Washington or what the massive political shift in the 50 states could bring, but with the Fed easing and plenty of cash on the sidelines, don't get too bearish and consider buying stocks on weakness.

November 10, 2010

DJIA: 11,346.75
S&P: 1,213.40

I Bought This T-Shirt at Marvin Gardens

One of the best sermons I have ever heard was a message about the board game Monopoly. The message title was "It All Goes Back In the Box," by John Ortberg. I think about that phrase and I wonder if Ben Bernanke and the Federal Reserve have a plan for the massive printing of money announced last Wednesday. Think of QE2 as Monopoly, and the printed money to be released into our economy is to help build houses and motels and generally create economic conditions conducive to growing an economy. But, unlike the U.S. economy, at the conclusion of Monopoly, the money and board pieces all go back in the box; no one gets hurt and the game is simply over. We can't say that about real life and consequences of QE2.

We have said before there are three things a nation can do to correct its spiraling debt problems: (1.) Default on its debt. (2.) Default on its people. Or (3.) Monetize the debt by printing money. Clearly, the Federal Reserve and this administration are taking us down the very risky and potentially dangerous path of monetization. Here is a very simple economic principle; If you print more money, it becomes less valuable and creates higher inflation in the long run. The late Milton Friedman said, "When a country starts on an inflationary episode, the initial effects seem good." A 17% rise in the S&P 500 since QE2 was suggested certainly has been good for stock investors, yet, will it last?

For the investor, the falling dollar against world currencies is the precursor to higher prices for goods and services here in the U.S. We remain steadfast in our belief that the greatest risk to investors will be inflation. Whether you buy CDs at the bank or invest in the stock markets, the greatest risk to your long-term well-being and purchasing power is the rising cost of living. It has been three decades since we have had to give serious consideration to this possibility. Inflation rarely creeps and slowly rises. My belief is when inflationary expectations reignite, prices will move up quickly, similar to the late '70s. You should be giving serious consideration to investments that have a hedging effect to keep pace with inflation.

But, there is hope and there is time to stem the tide of the Federal Reserve's own "irrational exuberance." We have experienced a two-year economic eclipse. The sunshine of growth and entrepreneurship was blocked out by the largest expansion of government-induced uncertainty since the Great Depression and perhaps ever. But, the clarion call of the mid-term elections is ushering in a sense of moderation and austerity; a belief in less government and more results. Voters spoke loudly and clearly that business as usual is unacceptable and the resiliency and determination that built America will lift this economy back to health once more. The question is, can the ineffective public policies and the massive printing of money all go back in the box?

Final Thoughts

In markets and politics, quickly rushing to a shallow and simple conclusion has become a sport in modern America. Often this leaves us with a faulty premise as we attempt to negotiate and make sense of the world around us. A wrong premise leads you down an errant path, encouraging you to follow your emotions or suspend the laws of economics, rather than engaging in an honest appraisal of current public policy, drawing on the lessons history offers.

My final thoughts are but scratching the surface of a topic that will be discussed, studied and written about for decades. In trying to find an effective way to describe the early years of the Great Recession, I believe you need to have thoughtful reflection rather than a simple expression of a shallow conclusion.

The Great Recession should be seen as an economic landslide. Landslides entail powerful exchanges of energy released in an instant, but this one had years of existing factors that created the tension that was ultimately released. The conditions that delivered the Great Recession were not created in the months leading up to the first domino of Lehman Brothers falling, but rather were the accumulation of excess debt from years of fiscal neglect. The many factors contributing to this landslide took decades to develop. The apparent stability on top of this shifting ground created the conditions for a disaster.

I don't know what specific financial trigger created this calamity. I will let historians draw that conclusion, but whatever it may be, it's clear this period of time will be seminal in the unfolding progression of our republic.

It is a key point to understand that the final chapters of this crisis are far from written. The unintended consequences have not been revealed, but with the extraordinary measures our government has taken, it would be naive to believe that there will be no consequences following the triage treatment our economy received during the last two years.

Unfortunately, investors have been presented with a set of circumstances that have made the markets more volatile and moving forward certainly entails increasing risk to be considered. Perhaps the most daunting piece of the investment puzzle will be the extended period of low returns on what historically has been safe money. For millions of retirees who have been and will continue to be dependent on these safe investments for income, the years ahead will most likely be treacherous. From lower interest rates to the devaluation of the purchasing power through inflation, "safe investments" will be in the eye of the beholder going forward.

On the political front, it will take courageous leadership to bridge the Grand Canyon-size divide our political parties have created. Intuitively, the American people know that the accumulation of government debt and the growth of entitlement programs must be reformed; they also know sooner is better than later, as the numbers are staggering. Unfortunately, the 2012 presidential election will delay bold action being taken on these critical issues of our time.

We won't know how indelible the recent financial events have been until enough time has passed and the dust of reconstruction settles. When we reflect back on the stock market crash of 1987, we remember that, at the time, it seemed history-altering. But, what we didn't know was what little weight it held in the fullness of history. Yet, it may be decades before future generations describe this era in a way that romanticizes the struggle, yet preserves the exceptionalism America has always claimed for itself.

I am confident that we will appreciate our resilience and our faith will be strengthened in an economic system the likes of which are unparalleled in human history.

In the times of historical transitions, I think it is normal and easy to underestimate the power of freedom. Yet free people, bolstered with a Constitution, provide one another with life, liberty, and the pursuit of happiness.

For the foreseeable future, the economy will likely experience slow growth and higher unemployment. I would expect to see the tension between deflation and inflation continuing, adding to the volatility investors have grown used to.

I don't expect to see consumer prices remain static. But as we muddle along I fully expect prices to have a bias toward the upside. The critical issue restraining a significant inflation episode remains a continued weak housing market, but having said that, we have experienced significant monetizing of our national debt. And creating money out of thin air creates some level of inflation.

The housing market needs time to heal; the deleveraging of the American economy has had structural implications for housing; we struggle to find a proper and accurate economic model to suggest when the final bottom will be reached. A side note: I wonder what the social cost of a broken housing market will mean for an ultimate recovery. With mobility restricted by home values and the inability to relocate easily, existing homeowners are disadvantaged from moving for better employment opportunities. This seems to be a quiet casualty of the financial crisis. Not since the Great Depression have we had millions of people feeling locked into their current situation – both in terms of economic flexibility and social choice. In other words, the land of opportunity is being restricted by a more stringent home ownership environment.

In the meantime, I do not expect to see the tide take all boats higher. But, I do expect that well-managed companies will find ways to be creative and innovative with an uncanny ability to increase their productivity, despite the economic landscape or government missteps.

As the events chronicled in this book begin to fade, we find ourselves negotiating an extremely polarized political landscape. A contentious debt ceiling debate in Congress during the summer of 2011, and the subsequent downgrade of long-term U.S. sovereign debt by Standard & Poor's once again drew sharp lines of division between believers in rival economic philosophies. That symptom of paralytic polarization will continue to reverberate, adding to the anxiety and trauma investors have been trying to put behind them.

By the end of summer 2011, we all understood the need for the reduction of debt on a global scale is an extension of the over-leverage we saw in corporations in 2007 and 2008, when private debt was replaced by public debt. This leverageed condition, now affecting the Eurozone and the United States will likely be a drag on economic growth for the foreseeable future, and will limit policy makers in their attempt to stimulate their slow growth economies.

The disaster and uncertainty that was a result of the train leaving the track will continue for a long time. Unless the nation unifies behind a leader who knows how easy it is for an economy – even one strong enough to drive the world's fortunes – to derail when the distractions of narrow politics and blind constituencies block the way, we'll find ourselves traveling in a circle – raising debt, flying off the rails, failing again and again, and going nowhere in particular.

The Great Recession has been a deep well of despair and regrets. Yet I believe our best days are still ahead of us. The American people will persevere. Our history is filled with dire times and little hope, but hope remained alive. We nourished hope with pragmatism and optimism and eventually America prospered once again. So it shall be again.

Proverbs 10:22
The blessing of the Lord brings wealth
And he adds no trouble to it.

Connect With Kevin Clark

On The Web:

www.economictrainwreck.com

By Mail:

99 E. 8th Street, Suite 400

Holland, MI 49423

By Phone:

(616) 395-4131

On Twitter:

http://twitter.com/EconTrainWreck

On LinkedIn:

http://www.linkedin.com/in/kevinclark1

At The Office:

ZICHTERMAN & CLARK
CAPITAL MANAGEMENT

www.zccapital.com

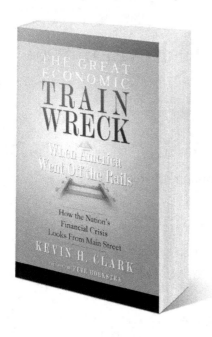

How can you use this book?

MOTIVATE

EDUCATE

THANK

INSPIRE

PROMOTE

CONNECT

Why have a custom version of *The Great Economic Train Wreck*?

- Build personal bonds with customers, prospects, employees, donors, and key constituencies

- Develop a long-lasting reminder of your event, milestone, or celebration

- Provide a keepsake that inspires change in behavior and change in lives

- Deliver the ultimate "thank you" gift that remains on coffee tables and bookshelves

- Generate the "wow" factor

Books are thoughtful gifts that provide a genuine sentiment that other promotional items cannot express. They promote employee discussions and interaction, reinforce an event's meaning or location, and they make a lasting impression. Use your book to say "Thank You" and show people that you care.